HEALTH CARE

THE ILAN STAVANS LIBRARY OF LATINO CIVILIZATION

HEALTH CARE

Edited by Ilan Stavans

 GREENWOOD

AN IMPRINT OF ABC-CLIO, LLC
Santa Barbara, California • Denver, Colorado • Oxford, England

Library of Congress Cataloging-in-Publication Data

Health care / edited by Ilan Stavans.
     p. cm. — (The Ilan Stavans library of Latino civilization)
   Includes bibliographical references and index.
   ISBN 978-0-313-36490-7 (hard copy : alk. paper) — ISBN 978-0-313-36491-4 (ebook : alk. paper)
  1. Hispanic Americans—Health and hygiene. 2. Hispanic Americans—Medical care. I. Stavans, Ilan.
   RA448.5.H57H385 2010
   362.108968'073—dc22

                                                    2009047444

13   12   11   10   9   1   2   3   4   5

This book is also available on the World Wide Web as an eBook.
Visit www.abc-clio.com for details.

ABC-CLIO, LLC
130 Cremona Drive, P.O. Box 1911
Santa Barbara, California 93116-1911

This book is printed on acid-free paper ∞
Manufactured in the United States of America

Contents

SERIES FOREWORD

The book series *The Ilan Stavans Library of Latino Civilization*, the first of its kind, is devoted to exploring all the facets of Hispanic civilization in the United States, with its ramifications in the Americas, the Caribbean Basin, and the Iberian Peninsula. The objective is to showcase its richness and complexity from a myriad perspective. According to the US Census Bureau, the Latino minority is the largest in the nation. It is also the fifth largest concentration of Hispanics in the globe.

One out of every seven Americans traces his or her roots to the Spanish-speaking world. Mexicans make up about 65% of the minority. Other major national groups are Puerto Ricans, Cubans, Dominicans, Ecuadorians, Guatemalans, Nicaraguans, Salvadorans, and Colombians. They are either immigrants, descendants of immigrants, or dwellers in a territory (Puerto Rico, the Southwest) having a conflicted relationship with the mainland US As such, they are the perfect example of *encuentro*: an encounter with different social and political modes, an encounter with a new language, and encounter with a different way of dreaming.

The series is a response to the limited resources available and the abundance of stereotypes, which are a sign of lazy thinking. The 20th century Spanish philosopher José Ortega y Gasset, author of *The Revolt of the Masses*, once said: "By speaking, by thinking, we undertake to clarify things, and that forces us to exacerbate them, dislocate them, schematize them. Every concept is in itself an exaggeration." The purpose of the series is not to clarify but to complicate our understanding of Latinos. Do so many individuals from different national, geographic, economic, religious, and ethnic backgrounds coalesce as an integrated whole? Is there an *unum* in the *pluribus*?

Baruch Spinoza believed that every thing in the universe wants to be preserved in its present form: a tree wants to be a tree, and a dog a dog. Latinos in the United States want to be Latinos in the United States—no easy task, and therefore an intriguing one to explore. Each volume of the series contains an assortment of approximately a dozen articles, essays and interviews by journalists and specialists in their respective fields, followed by a bibliography of important resources on the topic. Their compilation is designed to generate debate and foster research: to complicate our knowledge. Every attempt is made to balance the ideological viewpoint of the authors. The target audience is students, specialists, and the lay reader. Themes will range from politics to sports, from music to cuisine. Historical periods and benchmarks like the Mexican War, the Spanish American War, the Zoot Suit Riots, the Bracero Program, and the Cuban Revolution, as well as controversial topics like Immigration, Bilingual Education, and Spanglish will be tackled.

Democracy is able to thrive only when it engages in an open, honest exchange of information. By offering diverse, insightful volumes about Hispanic life in the United States and inviting people to engage in critical thinking, *The Ilan Stavans Library of Latino Civilization* seeks to open new vistas to appreciate the fastest growing, increasingly heterogeneous minority in the nation—to be part of the *encuentro*.

Ilan Stavans

PREFACE

Upon being diagnosed with cancer, a friend of mine from a small village in Guatemala who immigrated to the United States refused to visit the doctor again. She maintained that from the moment she entered the clinic and through the exams she was asked to submit to, she felt her privacy was invaded. No matter how insistent her friends were that she needed to pursue a cancer treatment, my friend resisted the idea. At first she sought help in a *botánica* and then she visited a *santero*, even though the practice didn't have any direct connection to her heritage. While the cancer receded temporarily, she died at age fifty-two, all alone because her family in Guatemala was unable to collect the necessary money to visit her.

The memory of her death haunts me. Not only was there a severe language barrier between my friend and the medical profession (in spite of my attending several appointments with her and the effort by the staff to find translators) but she was also misunderstood at the deepest cultural level. Her view of life was shaped in Guatemala, but her embrace of death took place in the United States. An abyss separated the two.

Among the most urgent issues affecting Latinos is the understanding of their health by the medical profession and the education Latinos need to obtain in order to adapt to ways of thinking and feeling in the Anglo world. How does their metabolism differ from that of other ethnic groups? What kind of nosology is needed to diagnose Hispanic disease? In what way should psychiatry accommodate their needs? What types of medicine and health-care services does this population prefer? And how should language barriers be sorted out so as not to undermine the health provider/patient relationship?

I have gathered in this volume seven studies of Latinos ranging from child care to sexuality and psychiatry. I have included studies that respond to reports that Hispanics are in worse health than whites; on the access to health care by immigrant families; on the use of herbs and plants in New York City; on the differences between being overweight among Mexicans, Puerto Ricans, and other Latinos; and on folk illnesses not recognized by medical practitioners.

The basic premise behind all of these is that Hispanics in the United States are not a homogenized group. There are dramatic differences along racial and class lines. Equally important is recognizing the divide between Mexican-Americans and Puerto Ricans in the mainland, for instance, as well as the idiosyncratic behavior that separates geographically the populations in the Northeast and in the Southwest in order not to fall into mistaken generalizations.

WHY DO HISPANICS IN THE UNITED STATES REPORT POOR HEALTH?

Sharon Bzostek, Noreen Goldman, and Anne Pebley

INTRODUCTION

The growth of the Hispanic population in the United States over the past 30 years has generated a large body of research on Hispanic health. Most of this research focuses on the "Hispanic paradox," i.e., the observation that Hispanics have lower mortality than non-Hispanic whites at most ages despite their lower average socioeconomic status (SES) (Franzini, Ribble, and Keddie 2001; Morales, Lara, Kington, Valdez, and Escarce 2002; Williams 2001). Hispanics as a group are also more likely to have healthier behaviors; for example, compared to non-Hispanic whites, they are less likely to use alcohol and to smoke (Morales et al. 2002; National Center for Health Statistics, Centers for Disease Control and Prevention 2002), more likely to eat high fiber and high protein diets, and more likely to have occupations involving physical activity (Morales et al. 2002).

Despite these health advantages, Hispanics, on average, report poorer self-rated health (SRH) status than non-Hispanic whites and members of other ethnic groups (Arcia, Skinner, Bailey, and Correa 2001; Finch, Hummer, Reindl, and Vega 2002; Ren and Amick 1996). SRH measures an individual's assessment of his/her overall health status in terms of four or five adjectives: for example, excellent, very good, good, fair, or poor. White–Hispanic differences in SRH are particularly large for Mexicans and Puerto Ricans (Franzini and Fernandez-Esquer 2004), but are common to all Hispanic groups, even when SES, nativity, and other measures of health are held constant (Cho, Frisbie, Hummer, and Rogers 2004; Shetterly, Baxter, Mason, and Hamman 1996).

Ethnic differences in SRH are important for at least three reasons. First, SRH is highly correlated with clinical assessments, is predictive of subsequent

Sharon Bzostek, Noreen Goldman, and Anne Pebley: "Why do Hispanics in the USA report poor health?" first published in *Social Science & Medicine*, Vol. 65, Issue 5, 990–1003.

mortality even when objective health measures are held constant (Angel and Guarnaccia 1989; Idler and Benyamini 1997), and is strongly correlated with other health indicators and health behaviors (Franzini and Fernandez-Esquer 2004; Manderbacka, Lundberg, and Martikainen 1999). There are, however, potential problems with using SRH as a measure of health for Hispanic respondents. While the findings outlined above have been found to apply to Hispanic respondents in general (Angel and Guarnaccia 1989; Franzini and Fernandez-Esquer 2004; McGee, Liao, Cao, and Cooper 1999), the reliability of SRH may differ across Hispanic subgroups. For example, one recent study found that SRH is a weaker predictor of mortality among recent Hispanic immigrants than among long-term immigrants and native-born Hispanic respondents (Finch et al. 2002). One potential explanation for this finding is that a given level of health may be interpreted differently by recent Hispanic immigrants than by others. If this is the case, then the use of SRH as an overall measure of health is questionable, particularly in analyses of ethnic or immigrant status differences in health. Such questions about the reliability of SRH for diverse ethnic populations also have implications for other self-reported measures and for health questionnaires often used in clinical settings.

Second, individuals' assessments of their own health status may have important effects on their decisions about health care utilization and other behaviors. Thus, if Hispanics, *ceteris paribus*, view their own health more poorly than others, they may be more likely than other groups to seek health care or use self-care. However, the tendency for Hispanic individuals to seek higher levels of care due to poorer self-assessments of health is difficult to observe through comparisons of health care utilization rates, which are affected by factors other than self-assessments of health. For example, although research suggests that health care utilization rates are *lower* among Hispanics than whites or other groups (Dey and Lucas 2006), this discrepancy is most likely due to lower rates of health insurance coverage and more limited access to health care for Hispanics (Prentice, Pebley, and Sastry 2005) rather than to differences in perceptions about the need for health care. Even if Hispanics' self-assessments of health lead them to seek care in greater numbers than whites and other groups, their relatively low levels of SES and other obstacles to accessing health care may translate into lower utilization rates.

Third, examination of the reasons behind Hispanic–non-Hispanic differences in SRH may provide useful insights into social and cultural differences in defining health and illness. Understanding group differences in the social construction of health and illness can, in turn, improve the design of public health programs and the delivery of health care.

Previous research on Hispanic–non-Hispanic differences in SRH has been hampered by data and methodological limitations. For example, three prominent studies are based on exclusively Hispanic samples (e.g., Angel and Guarnaccia 1989; Arcia 1998; Franzini and Fernandez-Esquer 2004). Other problems include the lack of data on key variables such as language of interview, immigration status, duration of residence in the United States, mental health, and SES. In this article we test several hypotheses about why Hispanics and whites differ in terms of SRH, using information from the first wave of the Los Angeles Family and Neighborhood Survey (L.A.FANS–1). We extend previous work in this area in several ways: our sample includes both

Hispanics and non-Hispanics, we differentiate between household language and language of interview, we include a broad range of immigration-related variables, and we include measures of SES not available in most studies.

HYPOTHESES

We test three hypotheses derived from previous research on Hispanic–non-Hispanic differences in SRH. Our first hypothesis relates to Spanish language and acculturation and involves two interrelated arguments. One of these arguments is that poorer SRH among Hispanics is partially an artifact of differences in meaning between Spanish and English language versions of the SRH question (Franzini and Fernandez-Esquer 2004; Phillips, Hammock, and Blanton 2005). The usual translation of the English response categories (excellent, very good, good, fair, and poor) is *excelente, muy buena, buena, regular,* and *mala.* "*Regular*" in Spanish can mean "okay" or "fine" (but also "so–so"), whereas in English, "fair" clearly connotes sub par health. Angel and Guarnaccia (1989) also suggest that there may be language-related differences in "anchoring," e.g., *buena* or *regular* may be used to describe normal health in Spanish (or in respondents' countries of origin), while excellent and very good may imply having no health problems—i.e., normal health—in English (or in the United States).

The second aspect of the language/acculturation hypothesis is based on research suggesting that differences in SRH between Hispanics and others diminish as Hispanics become more "acculturated," or integrated into mainstream American society (Angel and Guarnaccia 1989; Arcia et al. 2001; Finch et al. 2002). Angel and Thoits (1987) describe ways in which Mexican culture may affect perceived health status through the recognition, interpretation, and reporting of physical symptoms and emotional states. Some research suggests that it may be socially unacceptable for traditionally-oriented Hispanics to boast or be optimistic about their health (Shetterly et al. 1996). Because of the importance of cultural influences, self-evaluations of health among Hispanics may vary with time spent in the US, age at immigration, and degree of integration into US society. For example, immigrants exposed to American culture at a younger age may evaluate their health in a manner more consistent with native born Americans, as the results of Angel and Angel (1992) suggest.

Several previous studies have explored the association between acculturation and SRH using language of interview as the primary measure of acculturation. However, an association between language of interview and SRH could be due either to translation problems, as discussed above, or to a more traditionally-oriented cultural understanding of health. In this study, we attempt to separate the effects of language and acculturation on SRH by using both respondents' reports about whether Spanish is the only language spoken in the household and the language of interview. Primary language spoken at home is often used by immigration scholars as a key measure of acculturation (Alba and Nee 2003; Portes and Rumbaut 2001). If the association between language of interview and SRH is due solely to different cultural understandings of health, then this should be captured in both the language of interview and the household language questions. If, however, the relationship between language of interview and SRH is stronger than the relationship between household language and SRH, this suggests that differences between the Spanish and English versions of the questionnaire are likely to be important determinants of SRH. Given the complexity of the acculturation process, we also use information about age at immigration and duration in the US as additional measures of integration into US society. We expect to find that both language of interview and other acculturation-related measures partially explain differences in whites' and Hispanics' SRH.

A second hypothesis is that poorer self-reports of health among Hispanics may reflect aspects of quality of life and SES which are inadequately measured in previous research. A number of studies have shown that educational attainment and family income are strongly associated with SRH among Hispanics (Arcia 1998; Ostrove, Adler, Kuppermann, and Washington 2000; Ren and Amick 1996). However, previous studies have rarely examined other aspects of SES, such as unemployment and health insurance coverage, both of which we consider in this study. Based on previous research in this area, we expect that controlling for differences in SES will reduce the gap between Hispanics' and whites' SRH.

Our final hypothesis is that health assessments among Hispanics are more likely to reflect emotional states than reports of health by non-Hispanics. Specifically, Angel and Guarnaccia (1989) suggest that Mexicans and Puerto Ricans are more likely to "somatize," i.e., to experience psycho-social problems, such as affective distress, in physiological terms. Previous studies of Hispanics have shown a strong association between perceived racism and SRH, depression, and mental health (Finch, Kolody, and Vega 2000; Finch, Hummer, Kolody, and Vega 2001). This hypothesis suggests that affective states, such as depression, may be more prevalent among Hispanics as well as more likely to affect SRH for Hispanics than for whites or others. While empirical research suggests that, as a whole, Hispanics do not have higher rates of mental illness than whites, there is some evidence that rates differ among Hispanics by degree of acculturation, with native-born and long-term Mexican immigrants more likely than newer immigrants to experience depression and other forms of mental illness (for a review of this literature, see US Department of Health and Human Services, Office of the Surgeon General, 2001). Although we are likely to find that differences in rates of mental illness between Hispanics and whites do not account for the ethnic gap in SRH, ethnic differences in how mental illness affects respondents' reports of their overall health may lead to poorer reports of SRH by Hispanics. Thus, we would expect differences in SRH between whites and Hispanics to decrease if depression is taken into account.

DATA AND METHODS

DATA

Our analyses use data from the first wave of the L.A.FANS–1, a survey of adults, children, and neighborhoods in Los Angeles County. The survey employed a stratified random sampling design which oversampled poor neighborhoods and households with children under age 18. Data were gathered from approximately 40–50 households in each of 65 census tracts between April 2000 and January 2002, yielding a total sample size of about 3,000 households. More than half of the sample was Hispanic (mostly of Mexican origin), and in-person interviews were conducted in Spanish and English. The L.A.FANS questionnaire was designed by a team of experts that was bilingual in English and Spanish. The questionnaire was developed simultaneously in both languages, and many questions were drawn from major US surveys (primarily the National Health Interview Survey, Panel Study of Income Dynamics, and National Longitudinal Survey of Youth), which had developed both English and Spanish versions of their questionnaires.

L.A.FANS–1 collected information about two types of adult respondents. First, one randomly selected adult (RSA) age 18 or over from each sampled household was interviewed. Second, for each randomly selected child in households with children under age 18, that child's primary caregiver (PCG), typically the mother, was interviewed. Response rates were 85% for the RSAs and 89% for the PCGs (Sastry, Ghosh-Dastidar, Adams, and Pebley 2003). In approximately 40% of households with children, the same individual was designated as both the PCG and the RSA. The analyses in this paper use both of these samples—RSAs and PCGs (mothers only)—and examine them separately because questions regarding depression differed between these two groups. For ease of description, these samples are sometimes referred to as the sample of adults (RSAs) and mothers (PCGs).

MEASURES

Outcome variable

The dependent variable for all analyses is a five-category measure of SRH status, with higher values representing worse health. All respondents were asked the following question: "Would you say your health in general is: (1) excellent, (2) very good, (3) good, (4) fair, or (5) poor?"[1] In this analysis, we treat SRH as a five-category ordered variable. In exploratory analyses not presented here, we also modeled SRH as a dichotomous measure of poor/fair vs. good/very good/excellent health, as is done in many other studies,[2] and found similar substantive results. SRH is a component of the SF-12 and SF-36 health surveys, which have been validated in diverse cultural and linguistic samples (Arocho, McMillan, and Sutton-Wallace 1998; Bennett and Riegel 2003; Gandek et al. 1998; Peek, Ray, Patel, Stoebner-May, and Ottenbacher 2004).

Ethnicity and immigrant status

Due to the relatively small sample sizes of nonwhite, non-Hispanic groups, this study is limited to Hispanics and native-born non-Hispanic whites (whom we refer to simply as "whites"). Respondents were considered to be of Hispanic ethnicity if they reported Latino as their only racial category, or, for those who reported more than one race, if they reported that their race was best described by "Latino/Hispanic/Latin American." Mexicans are the only group with a sufficiently large sample size to be distinguished from other persons of

Hispanic origin. Respondents who reported Mexico as their place of birth and all respondents who reported themselves as Mexican/Mexicano or Mexican American are considered to be of Mexican origin. Nearly three-quarters of the foreign-born Hispanics in the sample who were not born in Mexico were born in either El Salvador or Guatemala, and approximately 15% were born in either Honduras or Nicaragua. Most of the remaining foreign-born, non-Mexican individuals were born in South America. The analyses employ the following set of six mutually exclusive categories to simultaneously represent ethnicity, national origin, nativity status, and age at immigration: (1) Native-born non-Hispanic white; (2) Mexican foreign born, immigrated as an adult (after age 17); (3) Mexican foreign born, immigrated as a child (by age 17); (4) Mexican native born; (5) Other Hispanic, foreign born; and (6) Other Hispanic, native born. As described in more detail later, we also estimate statistical models using alternative characterizations of the Mexican foreign-born population in order to assess the potential impact of different measures of acculturation.

Other explanatory variables

All models include age and sex, along with the six-category variable denoting ethnicity and immigrant status. Although we are not able to control for clinical measures of health status as Angel and Guarnaccia (1989) do, our models include a number of other measures of health status to minimize the chance that unmeasured health differences between Hispanics and whites are the source of variation in SRH. We excluded non-serious health conditions because respondents' reports regarding the presence of these conditions are likely to depend heavily upon their access to and utilization of health care. Health-care access and utilization, in turn, are related to ethnicity and immigrant status. As a result, analyses presented here rely on health measures that we believe are the least likely to be misreported. We include two measures of anthropometry derived from self-reports of height and weight: overweight/obese (BMI of 24.5 or above) and height in inches. We also include respondents' reports of physical or psychological problems that limit their work. Respondents who have ever been told by a doctor that they have had a heart attack, cancer/malignancy, coronary heart disease or other heart problems, or chronic lung disease are considered to have a "serious condition." Finally, we include indicator variables for heavy drinking (having five or more drinks in a single episode at least once in the past 30 days) and current smoking, based on previous studies that link these behaviors to self-assessments of health.

In order to examine the hypotheses described earlier, groups of variables pertaining to (1) language/acculturation, (2) SES, and (3) depression are added successively to a model that controls for health status and health-related behaviors to assess the degree to which these variables account for ethnic differences in SRH.

Several variables pertain to the hypothesis about language and acculturation. Household language, reported in the household roster, denotes whether Spanish is the only language spoken in the respondent's household. A second variable examines whether the respondent's interview was conducted in Spanish. While both of these measures are thought to capture aspects of the degree of acculturation of the respondents, a stronger relationship between language of interview and SRH than between household language and SRH would underscore the importance of translation issues. As described above, our main independent variable incorporates another measure of acculturation: age at immigration for foreign-born Mexicans. We also examined several additional variables related to immigration status in an effort to further explore the effects of acculturation on SRH and to examine the robustness of our findings to different specifications of age at immigration. Because the sample size of Mexican immigrants is too small to consider more than one sub-division, we replaced the age at immigration variable presented in our tables (by age 17 vs. after age 17) with four alternative formulations of immigration status for foreign-born Mexicans: immigration by age 35, immigration by age 9, immigration before 1990, and documented immigrant. Each of these formulations was introduced into a separate model, with the remaining four categories of the ethnicity/immigration variable (and all other variables) unchanged. In essence, this strategy provided four alternative versions of the final model that differed only with regard to a dummy variable denoting immigration status. Undocumented status among Hispanic foreign-born individuals was determined by identifying individuals who are foreign born but report that they are not citizens, do not have a green card, have not been granted asylum, and do not have a visa or have an expired visa.

Our second hypothesis predicts that differences in SES account for part of the disparity in whites' and Hispanics' SRH. Variables measuring SES are educational attainment, family income, current employment status, and current health insurance. Data on educational attainment come from self-reports of education obtained in the United States and/or other countries. Because foreign and domestic education categories do not directly correspond, responses were coded into three categories: less than secondary education, secondary education, and some post-secondary education. Family income, imputed by the L.A.FANS project staff if the data were missing, is divided into quartiles, and employment status is based on whether individuals report that they are currently working. We also include whether the respondent reports currently having health insurance. In cases where the respondent did not provide a response regarding existence and type of insurance, this information was taken from the household roster.

Our final hypothesis relates to the role of depression in influencing Hispanics' and whites' SRH. Both RSAs and PCGs were asked to report if a doctor had ever told them that they had major depression. The measure derived from these reports, which is included in the analysis for RSAs, is problematic, both because those who were *diagnosed* with depression are likely to be a select group and because respondents may be hesitant to acknowledge this diagnosis. Thus, this measure may underestimate the true prevalence of depression. PCGs (but not RSAs) were also asked to complete the Composite International Diagnostic Interview Short-Form (CIDI-SF) Depression Inventory. For the sample of mothers (PCGs), we use a measure based on the CIDI-SF that denotes the probability that the respondent was depressed during the past 12 months.

STATISTICAL ANALYSIS

We use ordered logistic regression to predict SRH status for each sample. The standard errors in all models are adjusted for clustering of the sample by census tract. We estimate nested models in order to examine if and how the coefficients associated with ethnicity are altered by the successive addition of substantive groups of variables to the model. All models are unweighted but include the following control variables to adjust for the sampling design and non-response (Sastry and Pebley 2003): number of people in the household, presence and number of children under age 18, neighborhood size and poverty status.

As noted earlier, this analysis is limited to Hispanics and native-born whites. Respondents who have missing values for the outcome or any of the explanatory variables (with the exception of those with imputed income values) are excluded from the analysis: 14% of cases for the adult sample and 19% for mothers. The resulting sample sizes for analysis are 1,708 for RSAs (adults ages 18 and over) and 1,161 for PCGs (mothers of the randomly selected children). A total of 617 individuals belong to both of these samples.

Fewer than 2% of respondents in each sample have missing values for SRH. The explanatory variable with the highest percentage of missing cases is the indicator for being overweight/obese (9% missing for RSAs and 13% for PCGs). Respondents excluded because of missing values for SRH have characteristics that are largely similar to those with non-missing values, although those excluded due to missing values for one or more explanatory variables have worse SRH than those included in the sample for analysis.[3] We assessed the extent of potential bias due to missing values by excluding the indicator variable for overweight/obese from our final model and estimated the model on two samples: the analysis sample and a larger sample that includes the respondents who were missing information on this indicator. There were no differences in the substantive results.[4]

RESULTS

Tables 1 and 2 present descriptive statistics for the samples of adults and mothers, respectively. In each case, the small number of Hispanic native-born individuals who are not of Mexican origin limits the statistical power of comparisons involving this group.

As shown in Table 1, SRH varies considerably across our six ethnicity/immigration groups. The differences between immigrants and native-born persons are particularly striking. Overall, whites assess their own health more positively than do all three groups of foreign-born Hispanics. Native-born Mexicans generally have better ratings than their foreign-born counterparts. These patterns are even more prominent for the sample of mothers (Table 2).

Variation in the proportions reporting fair health (category 4) across groups provides preliminary support for the hypothesis that translation problems give rise to some of the discrepancies in SRH by ethnicity. In Table 1, about 8% of whites and 10% of native-born Mexicans report "fair" health, compared with 26–29% of foreign-born Hispanics. As noted previously, some scholars have speculated that, because of the differences in how respondents interpret "fair" in English in comparison with "regular" in Spanish, this response category may be viewed more positively by Spanish speakers. The fact that foreign-born Hispanics (who are the most likely to have been interviewed in Spanish)[5] are three to four times as likely as the other groups to report "fair" or "regular" health provides some evidence in favor of this hypothesis. We return to this issue in the discussion of our results.

Tables 3 and 4 present the odds ratios from a nested series of five ordered logit models for the samples of RSAs and PCGs, respectively. Since the outcome measure ranges from one (excellent) to five (poor), odds ratios above one indicate worse self-ratings of health, relative to the reference category. As suggested by the results in Tables 1 and 2, estimates from Model 1 for both samples indicate that, in the presence of only demographic control variables, all groups of Hispanics report worse health than whites ($p <0.05$, except for native-born non-Mexicans). The odds ratios are particularly large for foreign-born Hispanics. Foreign-born Mexicans in both samples have significantly worse self-ratings of health than do native-born Mexicans. Contrary to expectation, the differences between Mexicans who immigrated as children and those who immigrated as adults are small and not statistically significant. The odds ratios change relatively little after controlling for health status and health-related behaviors (Model 2), suggesting that measured differences in physical health status and health-related behaviors cannot account for Hispanics' poorer ratings.

For both samples, language of interview (Model 3) is significantly associated with SRH, whereas an indicator of whether the household speaks only Spanish is not. Respondents who were interviewed in Spanish report worse health than do those interviewed in English (an odds ratio of 1.7 for the RSA sample and 2.1 for the PCG sample, in contrast to odds ratios very close to one for the household language variable). These findings support the conjecture that translation issues, such as differences in meaning between the adjectives used to describe the various health states in Spanish vs. English, may underlie some of the ethnic differences in reporting of SRH. Inclusion of the language variables in Model 3 results in a substantial decrease in the odds ratios for foreign-born Hispanics.

In line with previous research and our hypothesis about SES, the estimates from Model 4 indicate that ethnic variation in SRH is reduced considerably by the inclusion of controls for SES. Among the various measures of SES, level of schooling is most strongly associated with negative reports of health, suggesting that low levels of education among Hispanics, particularly the foreign-born, partly account for their poorer reports of health. Employment is not significantly associated with SRH, being uninsured is significantly associated with SRH only for RSAs, and the association between SRH and family income is significant only for the top income quartile for RSAs.

Including measures of depression in Model 5—whether the respondent reported having been diagnosed with depression (RSA sample) or the degree to which the respondent exhibits symptoms of depression (PCG sample)—permits us to address the somatization hypothesis. We evaluate two components of this argument, each of which could result in ethnic disparities in reports

TABLE 1

Descriptive characteristics for sample of randomly selected adults (RSAs), by ethnicity and immigrant status

	Total	White NB	MX FB, imm. as adult	MX FB, imm. as child	MX NB	Other, Hisp, FB	Other Hisp, NB
N	1,708	510	419	241	238	256	44
% of total sample	100.0	29.9	24.5	14.1	13.9	15.0	2.6
Self-rated health status							
1: Excellent/excelente (%)	21.6	31.6[b,c,e]	12.4[a,d,f]	17.0[a,d]	25.2[b,c,e]	17.6[a,d,f]	20.5[b,e]
2: Very good/muy buena (%)	23.7	33.1	14.8	19.1	30.7	14.8	36.4
3: Good/buena (%)	32.1	24.5	39.9	35.3	29.4	34.8	29.6
4: Fair/regular (%)	18.9	7.7	29.1	25.7	10.1	27.7	11.4
5: Poor/mala (%)	3.8	3.1	3.8	2.9	4.6	5.1	2.3
Health status and behaviors							
Overweight/obese (%)	64.6	53.9	72.3	68.5	67.7	65.2	72.7
Heavy drinker (%)	16.6	17.7	17.0	18.7	19.3	9.8	15.9
Current smoker (%)	15.1	16.9	13.6	12.0	16.4	12.5	34.1
Health problem that limits work (%)	12.9	16.7	11.0	9.5	12.6	11.7	13.6
Reports Dr.-diagnosed serious condition (%)[g]	8.4	14.3	3.8	7.1	5.5	7.8	11.4
Mean self-reported height (inches)	65.6	67.6	64.8	64.7	65.6	63.8	64.9
SD	4.1	4.2	4.0	3.7	3.8	3.4	3.7

Household speaks only Spanish (%)	29.2	0.0	64.0	39.4	3.8	48.8	4.6
Interviewed in Spanish (%)	46.1	0.0	92.8	69.7	9.2	79.3	13.6
Socioeconomic status							
Educational attainment							
Less than secondary (%)	39.5	6.5	69.2	60.2	24.0	54.3	22.7
Secondary only (%)	18.8	14.3	20.8	20.3	21.4	19.5	25.0
Some post-secondary (%)	41.7	79.2	10.0	19.5	54.6	26.2	52.3
Currently employed (%)	67.1	68.8	63.0	67.2	74.4	62.5	72.7
Mean family income (thousands of $)	48.9	98.4	21.7	25.5	43.4	24.2	35.6
SD, in thousands	67.5	98.7	22.2	23.2	43.2	20.2	46.0
Currently uninsured (%)	37.3	10.4	60.4	51.5	17.2	59.8	29.6
Reports Dr.-diagnosed major depression (%)	5.9	8.8	2.6	4.2	5.9	5.1	15.9

Estimates are unweighted.

[a]Overall distribution of self-rated health significantly different from white non-H NB (p <.05).

[b]Overall distribution of self-rated health significantly different from Mexican FB immigrated as adult (p <.05).

[c]Overall distribution of self-rated health significantly different from Mexican FB immigrated as child (p <.05).

[d]Overall distribution of self-rated health significantly different from Mexican NB (p <.05).

[e]Overall distribution of self-rated health significantly different from other Hispanic FB (p <.05).

[f]Overall distribution of self-rated health significantly different from other Hispanic NB (p <.05).

[g]Includes heart attack, cancer/malignancy, coronary heart disease or other heart problems, and chronic lung disease.

TABLE 2
Descriptive characteristics for sample of mothers (PCGs), by ethnicity and immigrant status

	Total	White NB	MX FB, imm. as adult	MX FB, imm. as child	MX NB	Other, Hisp, FB	Other Hisp, NB
N	1,161	258	345	187	146	200	25
% of total sample	100.0	22.2	29.7	16.1	12.6	17.2	2.2
Self-rated health status							
1: Excellent/excelente (%)	18.4	36.1[b,c,d,e]	9.3[a,c,d,f]	12.8[a,b,d]	19.2[a,b,c,e]	14.5[a,d]	28.0[b]
2: Very good/muy buena (%)	21.1	31.4	10.7	21.9	35.6	14.0	24.0
3: Good/buena (%)	36.4	23.6	46.4	39.0	29.5	38.5	36.0
4: Fair/regular (%)	21.0	7.0	29.9	24.6	11.6	28.5	12.0
5: Poor/mala (%)	3.1	1.9	3.8	1.6	4.1	4.5	0.0
Health status and behaviors							
Overweight/obese (%)	63.2	42.3	73.3	73.3	63.0	63.0	68.0
Heavy drinker (%)	6.3	7.8	4.4	5.9	10.3	4.5	12.0
Current smoker (%)	9.0	17.8	5.8	7.5	10.3	1.0	32.0
Health problem that limits work (%)	8.3	10.5	6.7	5.4	9.6	10.5	4.0
Reports Dr.-diagnosed serious condition (%)[g]	6.3	10.1	4.1	6.4	4.8	6.5	4.0
Mean self-reported height (inches)	63.3	64.8	62.8	62.7	63.4	62.5	63.2
SD	2.9	2.6	3.1	2.6	2.5	2.8	2.2

Household speaks only Spanish (%)	32.6	0.4	64.1	34.8	2.7	44.0	0.0
Interviewed in Spanish (%)	54.7	0.0	95.1	69.0	11.0	80.5	4.0
Socioeconomic status							
Educational attainment							
Less than secondary (%)	43.3	6.6	66.1	62.0	20.6	53.5	20.0
Secondary only (%)	19.6	11.2	23.5	21.9	21.9	19.0	24.0
Some post-secondary (%)	37.1	82.2	10.4	16.0	57.5	27.5	56.0
Currently employed (%)	54.2	64.3	42.3	47.6	71.9	53.0	68.0
Mean family income (thousands of $)	49.5	116.6	23.3	26.6	55.6	27.1	31.3
SD, in thousands	68.7	106.9	22.6	28.9	58.5	21.6	20.0
Currently uninsured (%)	38.4	6.6	61.2	47.1	10.3	53.0	36.0
Exhibits symptoms of depression (%)	15.4	17.4	13.0	14.4	14.4	19.0	12.0

Estimates are unweighted.

[a]Overall distribution of self-rated health significantly different from white non-H NB (*p* <.05).

[b]Overall distribution of self-rated health significantly different from Mexican FB immigrated as adult (*p* <.05).

[c]Overall distribution of self-rated health significantly different from Mexican FB immigrated as child (*p* <.05).

[d]Overall distribution of self-rated health significantly different from Mexican NB (*p* <.05).

[e]Overall distribution of self-rated health significantly different from other Hispanic FB (*p* <.05).

[f]Overall distribution of self-rated health significantly different from other Hispanic NB (*p* <.05).

[g]Includes heart attack, cancer/malignancy, coronary heart disease or other heart problems, and chronic lung disease.

TABLE 3
Odds ratios for ordered logistic regression of self-rated health status (1 = excellent, 5 = poor), sample of randomly selected adults (RSAs)

	Model 1	Model 2	Model 3	Model 4	Model 5
Ethnicity/immigration (white native-born omitted)					
Mexican FB, imm. as adult	3.58**	4.00**	2.49**	1.67*	1.70*
Mexican FB, imm. as child	3.29**	3.10**	2.25**	1.59**	1.62**
Mexican native born	1.70**	1.59**	1.56**	1.39*	1.41*
Other Hispanic FB	3.26**	3.20**	2.16**	1.60*	1.63*
Other Hispanic NB	1.67^	1.26	1.21	1.05	0.98
Health status and behaviors					
Overweight/obese		1.52**	1.52**	1.58**	1.54**
Heavy drinker		1.12	1.12	1.08	1.07
Current smoker		1.25	1.27^	1.18	1.14
Health problem that limits work		7.73**	7.68**	7.21**	5.95**
Reports Dr.-diagnosed serious condition		3.45**	3.40**	3.27**	3.12**
Self-reported height (inches)		0.95**	0.95**	0.97*	0.97*

Household speaks only Spanish		1.11	0.98	0.98
Interviewed in Spanish		1.66**	1.42*	1.45*
Socioeconomic status				
Educational attainment (less than secondary omitted)				
Secondary only			0.56**	0.54**
Some post-secondary			0.51**	0.50**
Currently employed			0.97	0.98
Family income (bottom quartile omitted)				
Second quartile			0.95	0.96
Third quartile			0.87	0.90
Top quartile			0.59**	0.59**
Currently uninsured			1.34*	1.36*
Reports Dr.-diagnosed major depression				2.76**
N	1,708	1,708	1,708	1,708

**p <0.01; *p <0.05; ^p <0.10 two-tailed.
All models control for the respondent's age and sex, the number of persons and the number of children in the household, whether the household has children, tract size, and tract poverty. The standard errors in all models are adjusted for census tract-level clustering.

TABLE 4

Odds ratios for ordered logistic regression of self-rated health status (1 = excellent, 5 = poor), sample of mothers (PCGs)

	Model 1	Model 2	Model 3	Model 4	Model 5
Ethnicity/immigration (white native-born omitted)					
Mexican FB, imm. as adult	4.78**	5.09**	2.81**	2.08**	2.16**
Mexican FB, imm. as child	3.33**	3.18**	2.17**	1.58^	1.65*
Mexican native born	1.91**	1.86**	1.84**	1.75**	1.82**
Other Hispanic FB	4.06**	3.89**	2.38**	1.83*	1.83*
Other Hispanic NB	1.63	1.44	1.49	1.27	1.38
Health status and behaviors					
Overweight/obese		1.54**	1.53**	1.56**	1.51**
Heavy drinker		0.79	0.80	0.81	0.77
Current smoker		1.41^	1.48^	1.36	1.31
Health problem that limits work		13.61**	13.73**	14.00**	13.09**
Reports Dr.-diagnosed serious condition		3.52**	3.42**	3.41**	3.18**
Self-reported height (inches)		0.95*	0.95*	0.95*	0.95*

Household speaks only Spanish			1.03	0.92	0.94
Interviewed in Spanish			2.06**	1.68**	1.69**
Socioeconomic status					
Educational attainment (less than secondary omitted)					
Secondary only				0.49**	0.50**
Some post-secondary				0.49**	0.49**
Currently employed				0.94	0.94
Family income (bottom quartile omitted)					
Second quartile				1.15	1.18
Third quartile				1.11	1.10
Top quartile				0.76	0.75
Currently uninsured				1.21	1.19
Exhibits symptoms of depression					1.62**
N	1,161	1,161	1,161	1,161	1,161

**p <0.01; *p <0.05; ^p <0.10 two-tailed.
All models control for the respondent's age, the number of persons and the number of children in the household, tract size, and tract poverty. The standard errors in all models are adjusted for census tract-level clustering.

of SRH: (1) that Hispanics are more likely than whites to be diagnosed with depression/experience depressive symptoms; and (2) that Hispanics are more likely to lower their self-ratings for a given level of depressive symptoms. The estimates in Tables 1 and 2 suggest that, based on the two measures of depression available in L.A.FANS, most Hispanic groups are less likely to be diagnosed with depression and to exhibit symptoms of depression than whites. Similarly, the odds ratios in Tables 3 and 4 for Hispanic groups are slightly larger in Model 5 than in Model 4, reinforcing the finding that the poorer health reports of Hispanics are not due to their experiencing a higher prevalence of depressive symptoms or being diagnosed with depression more frequently. These findings are consistent with previous research that finds that rates of depression for Hispanics are not higher than those for whites (US Department of Health and Human Services, Office of the Surgeon General, 2001). In models not shown here, we examined an interaction term between ethnicity and the depression variables, but these terms were not significant in either sample. Thus, although the depression measures are significantly associated with SRH, we have no evidence that Hispanics are more likely than whites to either experience or somatize this form of mental distress.

The results from the additional models described earlier, in which we tested alternative specifications of age at immigration, documentation status, and duration in the US, are very similar to those presented in Tables 3 and 4: the differences in SRH between Mexicans who immigrated at younger vs. older ages, who immigrated less or more than 10 years prior to interview, or who were documented vs. undocumented immigrants were small and not statistically significant in the final models (results not shown here).

Despite the extensive set of explanatory variables included in this analysis, we have not been able to account entirely for poorer reports of health among Hispanics. Results from the two samples point to similar conclusions. In our final models (Model 5), all Hispanic subgroups except the small sample of non-Mexican native-born respondents report significantly worse health than whites. Although foreign-born Mexican respondents reported significantly worse health than their native-born counterparts in the initial models, these differences became insignificant after controlling for SES.

DISCUSSION

Using detailed data from L.A.FANS–1, we evaluated three hypotheses proposed in the literature as explanations for poorer self-ratings of health among Hispanics. Our results provide new insights into the validity of these explanations and suggest avenues for future research.

Our finding that Spanish language of interview, but not Spanish household language, is significantly associated with worse SRH supports the notion that translation issues between the Spanish and English versions of the SRH question give rise to some of the discrepancies. Although numerous studies have documented associations between language and SRH (e.g., Angel and Guarnaccia 1989; Franzini and Fernandez-Esquer 2004; Shetterly et al. 1996), these studies have been unable to distinguish between linguistic artifacts and cultural aspects of language. Although language of interview is likely to capture both acculturation and translation issues, the persistently strong relationship between SRH and the measure of language of interview (but not the household language variable) provides support for the proposition that respondents interpret the Spanish and English versions of this question differently.

Additional evidence for the importance of translation issues is provided by a closer examination of the distribution of SRH by ethnicity and language. In Table 1, we showed that foreign-born Hispanics are between three and four times as likely as other groups to report "fair" (or "regular" in Spanish) health. The corresponding differences for the adjacent categories of poor and good health are much more modest, suggesting that the differences in the reporting of fair/regular health are likely due to more than cultural factors. The distribution of SRH by language of interview (results not shown) provides additional support for the potential impact of translation. Clustering of responses on the category of fair/regular health (in contrast to the adjacent categories) is more prominent when we focus on respondents interviewed in Spanish (in contrast to those interviewed in English) than when we make the corresponding comparisons by the household language variable or by foreign/native-born status.

Despite our finding that Spanish language of interview was consistently associated with worse reports of SRH, none of our other measures of acculturation—household language, age of immigration, duration of residence in the US, and documented status—is significantly associated with SRH. This result appears to run counter to previous research suggesting that cultural factors have profound influences on the perception and acknowledgment of health problems (Angel and Thoits 1987; Shetterly et al. 1996). We speculate that the apparent lack of importance of acculturation variables, rather than indicating that cultural factors do not matter for respondents' SRH, may be the consequence of two counteracting processes that underlie immigrants' adaptation to life in the US: (1) changing cultural values that render Hispanics more likely to assess and report their health as good (i.e., as whites do); and (2) deterioration in actual health status, resulting from the adoption of negative health behaviors in US society, and from stress associated with perceived racism and lack of social and economic opportunity in the US (Finch et al. 2000; Franzini and Fernandez-Esquer 2004; Lara, Gamboa, Kahramanian, Morales, and Hayes Bautista 2005). These two opposing processes for immigrants' SRH could, in effect, cancel each other out.

Our second hypothesis was that differences in SES would partially account for the disparity between Hispanics' and whites' SRH. This hypothesis was confirmed by our finding that lower SES (particularly schooling) is associated with poorer SRH, and that adjustment for SES substantially reduces the differences between Hispanics, and whites' self-ratings of health. Controlling for SES also closes the gap between native- and foreign-born Mexicans' SRH.

The somatization hypothesis has received considerable attention in research pertaining to SRH among Hispanics, yet this hypothesis has not been adequately addressed in the previous literature. In particular, some of the most frequently cited studies (Angel and Guarnaccia 1989; Arcia 1998; Franzini and Fernandez-Esquer 2004) are restricted to Hispanic samples, rendering it impossible to determine the extent to which mental distress accounts for discrepancies in SRH between Hispanics and other ethnic groups. Our study demonstrates that, to the extent that mental well-being is reflected by the diagnosis of depression or the presence of depressive symptoms, the evidence does not support this hypothesis. Although respondents who report diagnosed depression or exhibit symptoms of depression also report significantly worse health, Hispanics are not more likely than whites to experience either of our two measures of depression or to give excessive weight to psychological problems in their self-assessments of overall health. Depression, however, is only one of many mental health conditions likely to be associated with somatization. Research in this area would benefit from the inclusion in surveys of scales specifically designed to measure somatization of mental distress, such as the Somatic Symptom Index developed by Escobar, Rubio-Stipec, Canino, and Karno (1989).

Although this analysis is based on an extensive array of explanatory variables, we are unable to account fully for the worse self-assessments of health among Hispanics. Similar results have been obtained in other studies. For example, Shetterly et al. (1996) found that, after adjustment for SES, mental and physical health, health behaviors, and acculturation scores, Mexican Americans were more than twice as likely as whites to report poor or fair health. Potential explanations include the argument that some aspects of health omitted from our analysis are thought to be worse for Hispanics than for whites—e.g., diabetes, HIV/AIDS, functional limitations (affecting mostly older persons), and clinical risk factors pertaining to the cardiovascular, metabolic, and immune systems (Crimmins, Kim, Alley, Karlamangla, and Seeman forthcoming; Franzini et al. 2001; National Center for Health Statistics, Centers for Disease Control and Prevention 2002; Williams 2001). In addition, ethnic differences may emanate from culturally influenced understanding and expressions of health as well as choices of reference groups that are not captured by the measures in this analysis, or from other unmeasured factors that are not related to cultural orientations but are correlated with both ethnicity/nativity status and SRH.

The first wave of L.A.FANS has several advantages over other data sets for examining ethnic disparities in SRH, including a large Hispanic and non-Hispanic sample and a rich set of variables on immigrant status, language, SES, and health. Nevertheless, this survey also has several limitations. First, because L.A.FANS–1 is cross-sectional, the associations examined here could be bi-directional. Second, although L.A.FANS–1 includes more extensive information on immigrant characteristics than most comparable surveys, it lacks detailed data pertaining to respondents' linguistic and social adaptation to life in the US. Third, because health information in L.A.FANS–1 is entirely self-reported, these data almost certainly reflect reporting biases that are associated with language and culture as well as differential health utilization rates. One important corollary is the absence in L.A.FANS–1 of measures of biological risk factors for common chronic conditions (e.g., hypertension and hyperglycemia).

A second round of data collection of L.A.FANS (L.A.FANS–2) is scheduled for completion in 2008. Using data from both waves will permit a longitudinal investigation of the correlates of SRH for whites and Hispanics that is less likely to reflect reverse causality. In addition, L.A.FANS–2 is collecting the following types of data that were not included in the first wave: a modified Marin acculturation scale on language use in a range of settings and the ethnicity of people with whom the respondent regularly interacts (Marin, Sabogal, Marin, Otero-Sabogal, and Perez-Stable 1987), questions pertaining to discrimination and racism, clinical measurements of risk factors for chronic illness, and vignette measures of perceived health status that attempt to measure and adjust for systematic differences among social groups in response anchoring and cut-off points. The vignette studies included in L.A.FANS–2 will be particularly beneficial to researchers interested in understanding cross-cultural variation in SRH. In addition to L.A.FANS data, qualitative interviews with individuals from diverse ethnic backgrounds could provide important information about the choice of reference groups and the influence of mental distress in self-ratings of health. Future research that enhances our understanding of how different groups evaluate their health will help us better understand ethnic and immigrant-status differences in health status and health care.

ACKNOWLEDGMENTS

The authors would like to thank Germán Rodríguez and Elizabeth M. Armstrong for their valuable assistance in preparing this paper. We also gratefully acknowledge funding for this study from the National Institute of Child Health and Human Development (R01HD41486, Neighborhood Effects on Children's Well-Being and 5P30HD32030) and from the National Institute on Aging through the Center for Demography of Aging (5P30AG024361). L.A.FANS–1 was supported by the National Institute of Child Health and Human Development (R01HD35944), with funding from the Office of the Assistant Secretary for Planning and Evaluation (OASPE) of the US Department of Health and Human Services, Los Angeles County, the National Institutes of Health Office of Behavioral and Social Science Research (OBSSR), and the Russell Sage Foundation.

NOTES

1. The Spanish version of this question is: "¿Diría que su salud en general es excelente, muy buena, buena, regular, o mala?"

2. Some studies (e.g., Ostrove et al. 2000; Franzini and Fernandez-Esquer 2004) maintain the full five category measure, whereas others (e.g., Ren and Amick 1996; Shetterly et al. 1996) transform the multiple categories of SRH into a dummy measure of fair/ poor versus good/very good/excellent health.

3. RSAs missing on one or more explanatory variable are more likely to be non-white, to live in Spanish-speaking households, to have been interviewed in Spanish, to have low levels of education and to be uninsured. They are equally likely, however, to have health problems such as a doctor-diagnosed serious condition, diagnosed depression, or a problem that interferes with work.

4. Results found using dummy flag imputation in lieu of listwise deletion are essentially the same as those presented.

5. The correlation between Spanish language of interview and being foreign born is 0.79 for the primary (RSA) sample and 0.78 for the mothers' (PCG) sample.

REFERENCES

Alba, R., and V. Nee. 2003. *Remaking the American mainstream: Assimilation and contemporary immigration.* Cambridge, MA: Harvard University Press.

Angel, J. L., and R. J. Angel. 1992. Age at migration, social connections, and well-being among elderly Hispanics. *Journal of Aging and Health* 4(4):480–99.

Angel, R., and P. J. Guarnaccia. 1989. Mind, body, and culture: Somatization among Hispanics. *Social Science and Medicine* 28(12):1229–38.

Angel, R., and P. Thoits. 1987. The impact of culture on the cognitive structure of illness. *Culture, Medicine and Psychiatry* 11(4):465–94.

Arcia, E. 1998. Latino parents' perception of their children's health status. *Social Science and Medicine* 46(10):1271–74.

Arcia, E., M. Skinner, D. Bailey, and V. Correa. 2001. Models of acculturation and health behaviors among Latino immigrants to the US. *Social Science and Medicine* 53(1):41–53.

Arocho, R., C. A. McMillan, and P. Sutton-Wallace. 1998. Construct validation of the USA—Spanish version of the SF–36 health survey in a Cuban-American population with benign prostatic hyperplasia. *Quality of Life Research* 7(2):121–26.

Bennett, J. A., and B. Riegel. 2003. United States Spanish Short-Form–36 Health Survey: Scaling assumptions and reliability in elderly community-dwelling Mexican Americans. *Nursing Research* 52(4):262–69.

Cho, Y., W. P. Frisbie, R. A. Hummer, and R. G. Rogers. 2004. Nativity, duration of residence, and the health of Hispanic adults in the United States. *International Migration Review* 38(1):184–211.

Crimmins, E. M., J. K. Kim, D. E. Alley, A. Karlamangla, and T. E. Seeman. Forthcoming. Is there a Hispanic paradox in biological risk profiles for poor health? *American Journal of Public Health.*

Dey, A. N., and J. W. Lucas. 2006. *Physical and mental health characteristics of US- and foreign-born adults: United States, 1998–2003.* Advance data from vital and health statistics no. 369, Centers for Disease Control and Prevention.

Escobar, J. I., M. Rubio-Stipec, G. Canino, and M. Karno. 1989. Somatic Symptom Index (SSI): A new and abridged somatization construct. Prevalence and epidemiological correlates in two large community samples. *The Journal of Nervous and Mental Disease* 177(3):140–46.

Finch, B. K., B. Kolody, and W. A. Vega. 2000. Perceived discrimination and depression among Mexican-origin adults in California. *Journal of Health and Social Behavior* 41(3):295–313.

Finch, B. K., R. A. Hummer, B. Kolody, and W. A. Vega. 2001. The role of discrimination and acculturative stress in the physical health of Mexican-origin adults. *Hispanic Journal of Behavioral Sciences* 23(4):399–429.

Finch, B. K., R. A. Hummer, M. Reindl, and W. A. Vega. 2002. Validity of self-rated health among Latino(a)s. *American Journal of Epidemiology* 155(8):755–59.

Franzini, L., J. C. Ribble, and A. M. Keddie. 2001. Understanding the Hispanic paradox. *Ethnicity and Disease* 11(3): 496–518.

Franzini, L., and M. E. Fernandez-Esquer. 2004. Socioeconomic, cultural, and personal influences on health outcomes in low income Mexican-origin individuals in Texas. *Social Science and Medicine* 59(8):1629–46.

Gandek, B., J. E. Ware, N. K. Aaronson, G. Apolone, J. B. Bjorner, J. E. Brazier, M. Bullinger, S. Kaasa, A. Leplege, L. Prieto, and M. Sullivan. 1998. Cross-validation of item selection and scoring for the SF–12 health survey in nine countries: Results from the IQOLA project. *Journal of Clinical Epidemiology* 51(11):1171–78.

Idler, E. L., and Y. Benyamini. 1997. Self-rated health and mortality: A review of twenty-seven community studies. *Journal of Health and Social Behavior* 38(1):21–37.

Lara, M., C. Gamboa, M. I. Kahramanian, L. S. Morales, and D. E. Hayes Bautista. 2005. Acculturation and Latino health in the United States: A review of the literature and its sociopolitical context. *Annual Review of Public Health* 26(1):367–97.

Manderbacka, K., O. Lundberg, and P. Martikainen. 1999. Do risk factors and health behaviours contribute to self-ratings of health? *Social Science and Medicine* 48(12):1713–20.

Marin, G., F. Sabogal, B. V. Marin, R. Otero-Sabogal, and E. J. Perez-Stable. 1987. Development of a short acculturation scale for Hispanics. *Hispanic Journal of Behavioral Sciences* 9(2):183–205.

McGee, D. L., Y. Liao, G. Cao, and R. S. Cooper. 1999. Self-reported health status and mortality in a multiethnic US cohort. *American Journal of Epidemiology* 149(1):41–46.

Morales, L. S., M. Lara, R. S. Kington, R. O. Valdez, and J. J. Escarce. 2002. Socioeconomic, cultural, and behavioral factors affecting Hispanic health outcomes. *Journal of Health Care for the Poor and Underserved* 13(4):477–503.

National Center for Health Statistics, Centers for Disease Control and Prevention. 2002. A demographic and health snapshot of the US Hispanic/Latino population, prepared for the 2002 National Hispanic Health Leadership Summit. Unpublished manuscript.

Ostrove, J. M., N. E. Adler, M. Kuppermann, and A. E. Washington. 2000. Objective and subjective assessments of socioeconomic status and their relationship to self-rated health in an ethnically diverse sample of pregnant women. *Health Psychology* 19(6):613–18.

Peek, M. K., L. Ray, K. Patel, D. Stoebner-May, and K. J. Ottenbacher. 2004. Reliability and validity of the SF–36 among older Mexican Americans. *Gerontologist* 44(3):418–25.

Phillips, L. J., R. L. Hammock, and J. M. Blanton. 2005. Predictors of self-rated health status among Texas residents. *Preventing Chronic Disease: Public Health Research, Practice and Policy* 2(4).

Portes, A., and R. G. Rumbaut. 2001. *Legacies: The Story of the Immigrant Second Generation.* New York, NY: Russell Sage Foundation.

Prentice, J. C., A. R. Pebley, and N. Sastry. 2005. Immigration status and health insurance coverage: Who gains? Who loses? *American Journal of Public Health* 95(1):109–16.

Ren, X. S., and B. C. Amick. 1996. Race and self assessed health status: The role of socioeconomic factors in the USA. *Journal of Epidemiology and Community Health* 50:269–73.

Sastry, N., and A. Pebley. 2003. *Non-response in the Los Angeles Family and Neighborhood Survey.* RAND labor and population program working paper series 03-01. DRU–2400/7-LAFANS.

Sastry, N., B. Ghosh-Dastidar, J. Adams, and A. Pebley. 2003. *The design of a multilevel survey of children, families, and communities: The Los Angeles Family and Neighborhood Survey.* RAND working paper DRU–2400/1–1-L.A.FANS.

Shetterly, S. M., J. Baxter, L. D. Mason, and R. F. Hamman. 1996. Self-rated health among Hispanic vs non-Hispanic white adults: The San Luis Valley Health and Aging Study. *American Journal of Public Health* 86(12):1798–1801.

US Department of Health and Human Services, Office of the Surgeon General. 2001. Mental health: Culture, race, and ethnicity. A supplement to Mental health: A report of the Surgeon General. Rockville, MD: Substance Abuse and Mental Health Services Administration, Center for Mental Health Services.

Williams, D. R. 2001. Racial variations in adult health status: Patterns, paradoxes, and prospects. In N. J. Smelser, W. J. Wilson, and F. Mitchell (eds.), *America becoming: Racial trends and their consequences*, Vol. 2. Washington, DC: National Research Council, Commission on Behavioral and Social Sciences and Education, National Academy Press.

Understanding Differences in Past Year Psychiatric Disorders for Latinos Living in the United States

Margarita Alegría, Patrick E. Shrout, Meghan Woo, Peter Guarnaccia, William Sribney, Doryliz Vila, Antonio Polo, Zhun Cao, Norah Mulvaney-Day, María Torres, and Glorisa Canino

INTRODUCTION

Latino immigrants have better overall mental health than their US-born counterparts and non-Latino whites (Burnam, Hough, Karno, Escobar, and Telles 1987; Ortega, Rosenheck, Alegría, and Desai 2000; Vega et al. 1998), but the universality of this claim for all Latino subgroups has not been rigorously tested. Our findings from the National Latino and Asian-American Study (NLAAS) on the prevalence of psychiatric disorders among Latinos in the US indicate that foreign nativity is protective for some Latino groups (e.g., Mexicans), but not others (e.g., Puerto Ricans) (Alegría et al. 2007) and that protectiveness varies by disorder. Similar results were reported in the National Epidemiologic Survey on Alcohol and Related Conditions [NESARC] (Alegría, Canino, Stinson, and Grant 2006), suggesting that other factors besides nativity play a role in the likelihood of psychiatric disorders for Latinos.

This article seeks to identify risk factors for specific psychiatric disorders that may explain differences in nativity effects among Latinos. We report new results from the NLAAS that differentiate Latino respondents by country of origin and age at immigration. We hypothesize that past-year psychiatric disorders across Latino subgroups will be associated with differences not only

Margarita Alegria, Patrick E. Shrout, Meghan Woo, et al.: "Understanding Differences in Past-Year Psychiatric Disorders for Latinos Living in the US," reprinted from *Social Science & Medicine*, Vol. 65, Issue 5, 214–30.

in acculturation and enculturation processes, but also with factors related to family stressors and supports, contextual factors, and social status factors.

BACKGROUND

Complex factors may impact psychopathology across Latino ethnicity/nativity subgroups; differences could be due to variation in age, immigration experiences, acculturation and enculturation processes, family stressors, and perceptions of neighborhood and social status factors. Although Mexicans, Cubans, Puerto Ricans, and Other Latinos are usually grouped together as Latinos, their experiences both as immigrants and children of immigrants can be very different. For example, living in close proximity to Mexico and experiencing higher rates of immigration may reinforce Mexicans' cultural identity (Escobar, Nervi, and Gara 2000), while high rates of undocumented status might block opportunities for social mobility in the US (Powers and Seltzer 1998; Sullivan and Rehm 2005). Meanwhile, Cubans have the highest socio-economic status of all Latino groups, tend to remain Spanish-speaking in the US (Rivera-Sinclair 1997), and mainly reside within Cuban enclaves in Miami that assist in easing the transition to the US (Boswell, 2002; Hagan 1998). In contrast to the other Latino subgroups, Puerto Ricans have lived with more than a century of US influence, are US citizens, and are more likely to be bilingual and to have adopted many of the lifestyle patterns of US society (Guarnaccia, Martinez, Ramirez, and Canino 2005), including expectations for increased social mobility in the mainland US (Cortes, Malgady, and Rogler 1994). Other Latinos mainly include South Americans, Central Americans, and Dominicans, who come mostly as young adults in search of better employment opportunities or to escape violence (Pellegrino 2004).

ACCULTURATION, ENCULTURATION AND THE BICULTURAL MODEL OF ADAPTATION

Few psychiatric epidemiological studies of Latinos have investigated factors that account for the risk of psychopathology among Latino ethnicity/nativity subgroups living in the US, at least partially due to the challenge of disentangling the effects of acculturation from other risk factors (Rogler, Cortes, and Malgady 1991). Acculturation can be defined as "the acquisition of the cultural elements of the dominant society" (Lara, Gamboa, Kahramanian, Morales, and Bautista 2005), including norms, values, ideas, and behaviors. Since acculturation is an intangible process, researchers often rely on English-language proficiency as a proxy for cultural integration into US society (Blank and Torrechila 1998). Traditional acculturation measures have been criticized for their focus on a single variable with the extreme values (all Spanish/all English) representing high adherence to either the native or host-culture (Cortes 1994; Kim and Abreu 2001). This unidimensional model mistakenly assumes that the increasing acquisition of the dominant culture directly corresponds to systematic disengagement from the native culture (Rogler et al. 1991), thereby precluding assessment of the degree to which an individual is involved in each culture (Cortes 1994; Marin and Marin 1992).

To address this gap, the concept of enculturation has been introduced as part of a bicultural model. Enculturation is the process of preserving the norms of the native group (Kim and Ominzo 2006), whereby individuals retain identification with their traditional ethnic culture. Acculturation and enculturation can occur at the same time and can be measured separately (Kim and Ominzo 2006). Measures of Spanish language proficiency and usage and strong Latino ethnic identity are key indicators of close identification with Latino culture (Wallen, Feldman, and Anliker 2002), and therefore serve as proxies for enculturation. Different combinations of acculturation and enculturation (e.g., biculturalism, high acculturation-low enculturation, low acculturation-high enculturation, low acculturation-low enculturation) may lead to different adaptation experiences, and consequently different prevalence of psychiatric disorders. For example, bicultural individuals (those who have both acculturated to the dominant culture and retained ethnic identity through enculturation) may be able to contend with the demands of both cultures, leading to better mental health (LaFromboise, Coleman, and Gerton 1993). Both the acquisition of US cultural norms and values related to acculturation (Lara et al. 2005) and the maintenance of native cultural values, or enculturation, have been hypothesized to be linked to the mental health outcomes of different ethnic groups such as Native Americans, Asians, and Latinos (Kim and Ominzo 2006).

Immigration Factors and Family Stressors and Supports

Other immigration and nativity factors could also affect adaptation experiences. Specifically, those living in the US at an early age have more exposure to US culture at formative ages and may have weaker identification with native cultural values, such as strong family ties, that have been associated with better mental health (Finch and Vega 2003). From a developmental perspective, there are few expected differences between a US-born child of recent immigrant parents and a child who migrates to the US before the age of 6 (Suarez-Orozco and Suarez-Orozco 2001). Both would experience enculturating forces during their pre-school years, but would then integrate into US culture as they enter American schools (Suarez-Orozco and Suarez-Orozco 2001). Moreover, immigrants who come to the US before age 6 may confront significant pressure to acquire English as their dominant language (Suarez-Orozco and Todorova 2003), and this represents a strong cultural anchor for socially constructed meaning. "Because culture is a shared phenomenon passed from one generation to the next, language becomes the core medium of the communication and creation of culture" (Guarnaccia and Rodriguez 1996, 423–24).

Many researchers ignore the developmental relevance of age of immigration. We define immigration effects in a novel way. Instead of simply noting who was born in the US and who was born elsewhere, we propose to combine those immigrants who arrived before the age of 6 with those born in the US. The combined group is called "In-US-as-Child" (IUSC). Alegría et al. (2007) have documented that age 6 is, empirically, the best age cut point, as well as the one justified developmentally. The IUSC group is contrasted to immigrants who arrived after they already were in school. Later-Arrival Immigrants (LAI) refers to those who immigrated to the US after age 6.

In addition to a new look at the immigration experience, we evaluate the importance of social support processes for Latino groups. Several groups have argued that higher levels of family support among immigrants may also be associated with lower prevalence of mental disorders relative to US-born Latinos. For example, Hovey (2000a, 2000b) found that family dysfunction and ineffective social support were predictors of depression but the provision of emotional support from family seemed to ease stressful experiences of acculturation (Hovey and Magana 2002). However, there are few formal empirical tests on the role of family ties as a resiliency factor for Latinos' mental health, and most studies have only been conducted with Mexicans.

Moreover, disruption of family support networks (Rogler et al. 1991), increased intergenerational conflict, and heightened family burden in the form of excessive demands by extended family are hypothesized to be linked to psychiatric disorders. The socialization of young Latino children in US schools could be related to family cultural conflict, which itself may have an impact on the social support network. On the other hand, religious attendance, common among low-income Latino groups, might help minorities cope with the hardship of disadvantageous circumstances (Jarvis, Kirmayer, Weinfeld, and Lasry 2005) by establishing socially protective ties that buffer stressors.

CONTEXTUAL FACTORS

Regardless of nativity, Latinos (and other minorities) in the US may face additional life stressors linked to contextual factors that can influence the risk for psychiatric disorders. Unsafe neighborhoods, where Latinos are more likely to be living in comparison to non-Latino whites (Martinez 1996; Phillips 2002), may increase the likelihood of psychiatric disorders (Singer, Baer, Scott, Horowitz, and Weinstein 1998). Exposure to racial/ethnic-based discrimination (Finch, Kolody, and Vega 2000; Singh and Siahpush 2001) have been associated with negative health outcomes. Latinos—because of their skin color and as a result of their culture and language—are considered "persons of color" upon migration to the US mainland (Szalacha et al. 2003), leaving them vulnerable to experiences of discrimination that have been linked to poor mental health outcomes (Klonoff, Landrine, and Ullman 1999; Szalacha et al. 2003).

SOCIAL STATUS AND PERCEIVED SOCIAL STANDING IN THE US COMMUNITY

In addition, low social status (Alegría, Bijl, Lin, Walters, and Kessler 2000; Williams and Collins 1995) and subjective perceptions of low social status (Adler, Epel, Castellazzo, and Ickovics 2000) have been associated with higher risk of psychopathology. There is some evidence that once in the US, some Latinos experience a rapid transition in family structure from two- to one-parent families (Rumbaut 2006) and increased drug use (Hernandez and Charney

1998), with reports of marital disruption for Puerto Ricans and Mexicans but less data on whether this phenomenon applies to all Latino groups. Of all Latino groups, US-born Puerto Ricans have the highest rates of single-headed households and also the highest rates of substance use disorders (US Census Bureau 2000). We include marital status, employment status, income, education, and self-perceived social status as dimensions of social status following Marceau and McKinlay's model (Alegría, Takeuchi et al. 2004; McKinlay and Marceau 1999). These social status measures help describe where Latinos integrate into the hierarchy of US society and consequently can be used as proxies for the risk of psychiatric illness.

GOALS OF THE PAPER

As the preceding review suggests, there are a wide variety of potential influences on psychiatric risk and resilience among Latinos, and these influences might vary across subgroups defined by country of origin. The goal of this article is to examine these influences, paying special attention to the role of immigration experience within subgroups. To do this, we form eight strata of NLAAS Latino participants by crossing origin (Cuban, Mexican, Puerto Rican, and Other Latino) with a binary indicator of developmentally-informed immigration experience: LAI vs. IUSC. The latter group combines children who immigrated by age 6 with those who were born in the US, and we provide evidence supporting this combination. We examine the risk of these groups for depression, anxiety, and substance use disorders: disorders with relatively high prevalence and important public health and individual costs.

In addition to considering a developmentally informed definition of immigration experience, we incorporate ideas about enculturation when considering the experience of Latinos in the US. We differentiate the process of acculturation from that of enculturation in order to be able to conceptually and empirically capture the complex process by which immigrants may adapt to a new society. Including both acculturation and enculturation processes is particularly important for analyzing the factors associated with psychopathology (Kim and Ominzo 2006).

METHODS

SAMPLE

As described in detail elsewhere (Heeringa et al. 2004), the NLAAS is a nationally representative survey of English- and Spanish-speaking household residents ages 18 and older in the non-institutionalized population of the coterminous United States. Latinos were divided into four subgroups: Puerto Rican, Cuban, Mexican, and all Other Latinos. 2554 Latinos comprised the final sample with a response rate of 75.5%. This includes an NLAAS Core sample, designed to provide a nationally representative sample of all Latino origin groups regardless of geographic residential patterns; and NLAAS-high density (HD) supplements, designed to cover sample geographic areas with moderate to high density (≥5%) of targeted Latino households in the US. Weighting reflects the joint probability of selection from the pooled Core and HD samples providing sample-based coverage of the full national Latino population. The NLAAS weighted sample is similar to the 2000 Census in sex, age, education, marital status, and geographical distribution (data not shown) but different in nativity and household income, with more Latino immigrants to the US and lower-income respondents. This is consistent with reports of the undercounting of immigrants in the Census (Anderson and Fienberg 1999).

DATA COLLECTION

Data were collected by the Institute for Social Research at the University of Michigan between May 2002 and November 2003. Eligibility criteria for the Latino sample of the NLAAS included age (18 years or older), ethnicity (Latino, Hispanic, or Spanish descent), and language (English or Spanish). Professional lay interviewers administered the NLAAS battery, averaging 2.6 h. The Institutional Review Board Committees of the Cambridge Health Alliance, the University of Washington, and the University of Michigan approved all recruitment, consent, and interviewing procedures. A detailed description of the NLAAS data collection procedures are described elsewhere (Pennell et al. 2004).

MEASURES

The development of the NLAAS instrument involved creation of new measures, cultural adaptation of existing measures, and translation of most measures into Spanish. Some measures, such as family burden and discrimination, were adopted from the National Survey of American Life (Jackson et al. 2004) and the National Comorbidity Survey Replication (Kessler and Merikangas 2004). Key variables and scales with their psychometric properties are described in Alegría et al. (2004). Most measures were selected based on face validity, internal reliability, and use in other studies of Latino mental health, maintaining the items of the originators.

Demographic variables used in the analysis are *gender* and *age* (18–24; 25–34; 35–49; 50–64; ≥65), using comparable categories to those previously used in the literature (Capps, Fix, Ost, Reardon-Anderson, and Passel 2004). Individual immigration factors, such as *parental nativity for US-born* (whether one or both of respondent's parents were US-born, or both foreign-born) and *age of arrival of immigrants* (to US: 0–6, 7–17, 18–24, and 25+ years of age), are also assessed as variables linked to nativity that might influence experience of adaptation to US society. We used an *English language proficiency* scale (α = 0.98) as a proxy to measure the construct of acculturation. This scale assesses respondents' ability to speak, read, and write in English (higher scores indicate higher-level proficiency; Felix-Ortiz, Newcomb, and Myers 1994). Similarly, we used the *Spanish language proficiency* scale (α = 0.90) and the *ethnic identity* scale (α = 0.75) as proxies to measure the construct of enculturation. The Spanish language proficiency scale assesses respondents' ability to speak, read, and write in Spanish (higher scores indicate higher-level proficiency; Felix-Ortiz et al. 1994). The ethnic identity scale determines respondents' identification with, closeness of ideas about things, and shared time with members of their own ethnic group; with higher values indicating higher Latino ethnic identity.

To evaluate family stressors and family and other supports, we include three scales measuring *family factors* and one question evaluating *religious attendance*. The three-item *family support* scale assesses respondents' ability to rely on relatives by asking how often they talk on the telephone and how much they can open up to relatives ($\alpha = 0.71$). *Family burden*, a two-item measure, captures frequency of demands and arguments with relatives or children, developed by Kessler and colleagues (Pennell et al. 2004). The *family cultural conflict* scale consists of five items measuring respondents' frequency of cultural and intergenerational conflict with families (e.g., family interference with personal goals, arguments with family members due to different belief systems) ($\alpha = 0.91$). All scale scores shown in Table 1 were transformed so that their range was 0–1; hence, the scales represent the comparison of a subject with the highest possible score to a subject with the lowest possible score. Average scale scores were: 0.660 for family support, 0.307 for family burden, and 0.134 for family cultural conflict (with larger numbers respectively indicating more support, greater burden, and greater conflict). *Religious attendance* measured frequency of attendance at religious services (≥ 1 /week, <1/week, never). *Religious attendance* was classified as a support factor, since religious institutions have been shown to offer critical comfort to Latino immigrants by easing the transition to a new context and serving to link immigrants into US communities while remaining connected to cultural values and norms (Levitt 1998; Menjivar 1999).

Contextual factors include *perceived neighborhood safety* and exposure to *discrimination*. In the *neighborhood safety* scale, three items measure respondents' perceived level of neighborhood safety and lack of violence ($\alpha = 0.72$). Higher scores indicate a greater degree of perceived safety. Exposure to *discrimination* is a nine-item measure measuring frequency of routine experiences of unfair treatment (e.g., being treated with less respect than other people, having people act afraid of them; $\alpha = 0.82$).

Social status variables include *marital status* (married; divorced, separated, and widowed; never married), level of education (no high school (<9); some high school (9–11); high school graduate (12); some college (13–15); college degree or greater (≥ 16)), *annual household income* for the prior year ($\$0$–14,999; $\$15,000$–34,999; $\$35,000$–74,999; $\$75,000$), *employment status* (employed; unemployed; out of workforce), and *perceived social status*. *Perceived social status* is assessed by asking respondents to identify their social status relative to others in their US community, based on money, education, and job respect (Adler et al. 2000). Higher scores indicate higher levels of perceived social status.

Diagnostic measures for last twelve-month prevalence of psychiatric disorders were obtained using the diagnostic interview of the World Mental Health Survey Initiative version of the World Health Organization Composite International Diagnostic Interview (WMH-CIDI; Kessler and Ustun 2004) a structured diagnostic instrument based on criteria of the DSM-IV.

TABLE 1
Differences in unadjusted and adjusted[a] percentages/means by Latino subgroups[a]

	Unadjusted percentages or means					Adjusted percentages or means				
	Puerto Rican	Cuban	Mexican	Other Latino	Test of differences	Puerto Rican	Cuban	Mexican	Other Latino	Test of differences
Sample										
N	494	576	863	613						
Weighted %	10.1	4.6	56.5	28.8						
Demographics										
% Female	51.2	47.3	46.2	52.4	*	46.9	51.1	48.7	48.9	NS
Mean age	41.0	48.8	36.6	38.0	***	38.7	36.4	37.8	37.5	NS
Immigration factors[b]										
% US born	55.1	13.9	43.2	38.3	**	58.7	23.6	43.8	38.7	**
Immigrants: % age of arrival 0-6 years	10.4	9.2	5.1	8.3	*	10.3	12.3	5.2	8.4	**
Immigrants: % age of arrival ≥7 years	34.6	77.0	51.6	53.4	***	31.0	64.1	51.0	52.9	**
Acculturation factor										
% good/excellent English proficiency	69.5	40.7	45.7	56.6	***	62.3	63.0	45.9	60.7	***
Enculturation factors										
% good/excellent Spanish proficiency	68.3	86.6	69.4	73.1	**	70.4	83.9	69.8	72.6	NS
Mean Latino ethnic identity scale	0.785	0.850	0.783	0.754	***	0.798	0.819	0.785	0.746	**
Family stressors and social supports										
Mean family support scale	0.668	0.741	0.659	0.644	**	0.684	0.748	0.668	0.647	NS
Mean family burden scale	0.328	0.257	0.298	0.324	**	0.303	0.330	0.299	0.326	NS
Mean family cultural conflict scale	0.151	0.110	0.130	0.139	**	0.133	0.112	0.130	0.146	NS

% Religious attendance: ≥1/wk	31.6	21.3	33.8	34.6	NS	32.4	26.4	34.8	33.3	NS
% Religious attendance: <1/wk	39.9	47.4	50.1	45.3	*	38.0	46.9	49.0	46.2	Y
% Religious attendance: never	28.4	31.3	16.1	20.1	***	29.6	26.7	16.2	20.5	***
Contextual factors										
Mean neighborhood safety scale	0.654	0.787	0.718	0.694	***	0.660	0.758	0.718	0.690	*
Mean discrimination scale	0.193	0.088	0.162	0.168	***	0.192	0.138	0.159	0.173	NS
Social status factors										
% Married	39.6	56.2	57.1	45.0	***	39.9	52.1	58.0	45.4	***
% Divorced, separated, widowed	27.0	27.3	14.5	21.9	***	22.8	20.0	15.4	20.9	**
% Never married	33.4	16.5	28.4	33.1	*	37.3	27.8	26.7	33.7	*
% Employed	58.2	60.1	63.3	66.0	NS	56.8	68.6	61.0	67.2	NS
% Out of work force	35.2	35.2	29.8	25.4	NS	35.5	26.6	32.2	24.6	NS
% Unemployed	6.6	4.6	6.8	8.6	NS	7.7	4.8	6.8	8.2	NS
Mean years of education	11.7	12.1	10.0	11.6	***	11.9	13.0	9.7	11.6	***
Mean household income ($)	56,100	58,600	39,300	53,400	**	54,300	65,400	38,800	54,200	**
Mean perceived social standing scale	0.619	0.639	0.602	0.629	NS	0.633	0.661	0.599	0.635	*
12-month disorders										
% Any depressive dx	12.0	8.3	8.4	8.8	NS	9.8	8.1	8.7	7.8	NS
% Any anxiety dx	15.8	11.3	9.2	7.8	*	13.2	14.0	9.8	7.3	NS
% Any substance dx	3.4	1.7	2.9	2.9	NS	3.8	3.4	2.7	3.3	NS
% Any disorder dx	24.3	16.6	15.6	15.2	*	21.2	19.8	16.3	14.9	NS

NS, nonsignificant (p ≥0.05).

*p <0.05, **p <0.01, ***p <0.001.

a Adjusted by sex, age, nativity, and age of arrival of immigrants.

b Immigrant factors adjusted only for sex and age.

TABLE 2

Comparison of US born, immigrants with age of arrival 0–6 years, and immigrants with age of arrival ≥7 years[a]

	US born (1)	Immigrants age of arrival 0–6 years (2)	Immigrants age of arrival ≥7 years (3)	Test of (1) vs. (2)	Test of (2) vs. (3)
Sample					
N	924	203	1,419	—	—
Weighted %	41.6	6.8	51.6	—	—
Demographics					
% Female	48.6	49.7	48.3	NS	NS
Mean age	36.7	34.3	39.6	NS	***
Acculturation factors					
% good/excellent English proficiency	86.1	83.0	18.5	NS	***
Enculturation factors					
% good/excellent Spanish proficiency	55.1	77.1	80.6	***	NS
Mean ethnic identity scale	0.761	0.773	0.790	NS	NS
Family stressors and social supports					
Mean family support scale	0.686	0.663	0.633	NS	NS
Mean family burden scale	0.362	0.367	0.252	NS	***
Mean family cultural conflict scale	0.149	0.166	0.122	NS	NS
% Religious attendance: ≥1 wk	30.9	37.4	34.2	NS	NS
% Religious attendance: <1 wk	47.0	49.0	48.0	NS	NS
% Religious attendance: never	22.1	13.6	17.8	*	NS

Contextual factors					
Mean neighborhood safety scale	0.723	0.794	0.690	**	***
Mean discrimination scale	0.205	0.198	0.127	NS	**
Social status factors					
% Married	47.4	55.5	54.9	NS	NS
% Divorced, separated, widowed	20.6	17.5	17.5	NS	NS
% Never married	32.0	27.0	27.6	NS	NS
% Employed	64.8	65.6	63.1	NS	NS
% Out of work force	27.0	25.3	31.4	NS	NS
% Unemployed	8.2	9.1	5.5	NS	NS
Mean years of education	12.0	12.7	9.5	NS	***
Mean household income ($)	56,200	53,800	37,000	NS	**
Mean perceived social standing scale	0.627	0.682	0.595	***	***
12-month disorders					
% Any depressive dx	10.3	8.1	7.8	NS	NS
% Any anxiety dx	10.4	10.5	8.4	NS	NS
% Any substance dx	5.0	2.4	1.1	NS	NS
% Any disorder dx	19.2	18.1	13.5	NS	NS

NS, nonsignificant ($p \geq 0.05$).

*$p < 0.05$, **$p < 0.01$, ***$p < 0.001$.

[a]All factors except sex and age adjusted by sex and age.

ANALYSES

We compute percentages and means of key variables in two ways: unadjusted, and adjusted for gender, age, parental nativity of US-born, and age of arrival of immigrants. These analyses contrast Latino subethnic groups, then adjust in separate steps for immigration–acculturation–enculturation factors, family factors, contextual factors, and social status factors. Analysis of variables related to immigration experience required a special approach. Certain sources of variation are only meaningful for subsets of participants. For example, age of immigration is only meaningful for immigrants. Birth place of parents will only have meaningful variation among US-born respondents. To allow comparisons across both immigrants and US-born, we chose to use group averages as the reference group for contrasts involving parental nativity and age of immigration. Specifically, we contrasted US-born respondents with both parents US-born to the average of the IUSC group, and we contrasted US-born respondents with both parents foreign-born to the same IUSC average. Immigrants who arrived at age 0–6 were contrasted to the IUSC average. Similarly, the three age groups of immigration associated with risk (7–17, 18–24, 25+) were contrasted to the average of the LAI group. Two of these six contrasts are redundant with the others, but we provide them all for descriptive purposes.

We also compared unadjusted and adjusted 12-month prevalence of DSM-IV disorders focusing on composite diagnostic categories of *any depressive disorder* (dysthymia and/or major depressive episode), *any anxiety disorder* (agoraphobia, social phobia, generalized anxiety disorder, post traumatic stress, and/or panic disorder), *any substance disorder* (drug abuse, drug dependence, alcohol abuse, and/or alcohol dependence) or *any disorder across subgroups* (any depressive, any anxiety, any substance disorder). Unadjusted and adjusted contrasts across the four Latino subethnicity groups (see Table 1) are tested using the Rao-Scott adjustments (Rao and Scott 1984) provided by the STATA survey command for categorical variables and tests of mean value differences for continuous variables. This first set of comparisons reveals the differences across Latino subethnicity. We also contrasted Latinos by nativity and age of arrival to the US (before age 6 or after age 6, in Table 2) in the factors of interest. This second set of comparisons helps clarify the delineation of our nativity groups based on age of arrival to the US, with both sets of comparisons establishing the eight Latino ethnicity/nativity subgroups.

Logistic regression models assess whether proposed factors explain differences in risk of depressive, anxiety, and substance disorders among the eight Latino ethnicity/nativity subgroups. We constructed five hierarchical models that successively adjusted for the immigration and cultural measures described above. To conserve space, we present only Model 1 and the Final Model in this article, but the complete set is available from the authors. Model 1 includes indicators for ethnicity/nativity subgroups and adjusts only for age and sex. The second through fourth models successively add immigration, acculturation, and enculturation factors, then family stressors and support factors (including religious attendance), and then contextual factors (e.g., perceived neighborhood safety and discrimination). The Final Model includes all of these variables and social status factors (e.g., marital status, employment status, education, income, and self-perceived social standing). To maximize the precision of estimates, we used all available observations for each step. As additional variables were added, sample size declined slightly because of missing values. To be sure that difference in results between Model 1 and the Final Model are not due to changes in sample size, we conducted a sensitivity analysis that restricts the samples for Model 1 to be the same as that of the Final Model. Results are consistent with those reported here. Stata statistical software (Stata Corporation 2004) survey analysis procedures, which account for the complex sampling design, were used to conduct all analyses.

RESULTS

Differences by Latino subethnicity

Table 1 depicts the variation in factors related to psychopathology risk, stratified by Latino subethnicity. Looking only at unadjusted values, we observe that more than half of Puerto Ricans are born in the mainland US. Puerto Ricans have high levels of family cultural conflict, perceived exposure to discrimination, and good or excellent English language proficiency; low levels of perceived neighborhood safety; and increased likelihood of marital disruption and of any 12-month disorders compared to other Latino subgroups. Cubans tend to be mostly late-arrival immigrants, arriving in the US after age 6. They report high levels of family support, Latino ethnic identity, and good or excellent Spanish language proficiency; and low levels of family burden and family cultural conflict in comparison to other Latino groups. Mexicans on average are young, with low mean household incomes. They are less likely to be divorced, and report low rates of any 12-month disorders. Other Latinos are similar to Mexicans in terms of level of family cultural conflict, perceived exposure to discrimination, and level of perceived neighborhood safety. They report the lowest rates of any anxiety and any 12-month disorder.

Our findings for the unadjusted percentages/means in Table 1 show how Latino subethnic groups are significantly different in demographic, immigration, acculturation, enculturation, family, contextual and social status factors. These results also demonstrate that subethnic groups vary significantly in prevalence of anxiety and any psychiatric disorder. However, these differences diminish and are no longer statistically significant once we adjust for differences in age, sex, nativity, and age of arrival for immigrants.

Differences by nativity and age of arrival to the US

To clarify the rationale for the delineation of our nativity groups, we present the findings that led us to combine immigrants who arrived before age 6 together with the US-born. Table 2 shows demographic and risk comparisons of US-born and immigrant respondents, with immigrant respondents split into two categories: immigrants who arrived in the US before, and after, age 6. The majority of the sample consists of LAI who immigrated after age 6 (51.6%), whereas 41.6% are US-born and 6.8% arrived in the US between the ages of

0–6. Although the last group speaks Spanish as well as LAIs, they are much more like the US-born in terms of English fluency. This reflects the developmental salience of immigration before starting school.

In addition to language comparisons, young immigrants differed from LAI in seven other risk/demographic variables (age, family burden, neighborhood safety, reported level of discrimination, education, income, and social standing). In contrast, young immigrants only differed from the US-born in three variables (other than Spanish proficiency): religious attendance, neighborhood safety, and social standing. For the latter two variables, young immigrants were more advantaged than the US-born, but even more advantaged than LAI. These findings provide empirical support for the formation of the IUSC group, as a combination of US-born and young immigrants, in contrast to LAI.

REGRESSION MODELS FOR DEPRESSIVE, ANXIETY, AND SUBSTANCE USE DISORDERS

Table 3 summarizes the results of logistic regression models to study factors that contribute to the explanation of risk for depressive, anxiety, and substance use disorders. The first block of information shows odds ratios (OR) for Latino subgroups relative to IUSC Mexicans, using the seven pair-wise comparisons with the IUSC Mexican reference group. The second block (shaded dark grey) reports derived odds ratios for LAI vs. IUSC for each subethnicity. These odds ratios are derived from contrasts of the subethnicity/nativity terms shown above them, and are not additional terms in the model. These derived estimates are generated using the lincom command in STATA 9, which computes point estimates and confidence intervals from linear combinations of coefficients. They are presented to facilitate inferences about LAI in each subethnic group. Three sets of columns in the Table show results for depressive, anxiety, and substance use disorders, and in each set we present Model 1 (adjusted for only age and sex) and the Final model (adjusted for all available measures). The bottom rows of Table 3 show results from the three omnibus statistical tests for nativity and subethnicity differences for each model that are computed as adjusted Wald tests. The first row shows the test of any difference among eight ethnicity/nativity subgroups, such as whether differences exist between LAI Puerto Ricans and IUSC Mexicans. The second row gives the test of LAI vs. IUSC difference, stratified by subethnicity, such as whether differences exist between LAI Cubans and IUSC Cubans. The third row shows the test of whether the immigration (IUSC vs. LAI) variation is significantly different across the four pairs of Latino subgroups (Puerto Ricans, Cubans, Mexicans, and Other Latinos).

DEPRESSIVE DISORDERS

The first columns of Table 3 show that two of the seven Latino subgroups are significantly different from IUSC Mexicans in the risk of past-year depressive disorders, after age and gender adjustments. IUSC Cubans and LAI Mexicans reported significantly lower prevalence of depressive disorders than IUSC Mexicans (IUSC Cubans: OR = 0.4, p <0.05; LAI Mexicans: OR = 0.5, p <0.001)

(Model 1). The bottom of Table 3 reports omnibus tests. All three show significance at the p <0.05 level in Model 1 (with age and gender adjustments). The first verifies that subethnicity groups differ from each other, and the second indicates that LAIs tend to differ from IUSCs within each subethnicity. The third test reveals that immigration effects vary from one subethnic group to the next.

In the Final Model, which was adjusted for a variety of effects shown in Table 3, none of the omnibus tests showed significance. In this model, the terms that increased risk for depressive disorders include: family burden (OR = 3.0, p <0.05); family cultural conflict (OR = 2.7, p <0.01); being divorced, separated, or widowed compared to being married (OR = 2.0, p <0.001); and being out of the work force compared to being employed (OR = 1.8, p <0.01). The terms that seemed to be protective for depressive disorders include perceived neighborhood safety (OR = 0.3, p <0.01) and perceived high social standing in the US community (OR = 0.2, p <0.05).

ANXIETY DISORDERS

The risk for anxiety disorders appears no different for LAI relative to IUSC Latinos, after age and sex adjustments (Model 1 in the shaded block of Table 3). After adjusting for all other factors in the Final Model, IUSC Other Latinos reported a significantly lower prevalence of anxiety disorders than IUSC Mexicans (OR = 0.4, p <0.05). In the Final Model, those with both parents foreign-born have lower risk for anxiety disorders (OR = 0.6, p <0.05) as compared to the average IUSC participant. This is consistent with all the models (results not shown). Risk factors for past-year anxiety disorders include: family burden (OR = 6.0, p <0.001); family cultural conflict (OR = 3.2, p <0.01); perceived discrimination (OR = 4.9, p <0.05); never being married compared to being married (OR = 1.6, p <0.05); and being out of the work force compared to being employed (OR = 2.7, p <0.001). Similar to the findings for depressive disorders, self-perceived high social standing is significantly associated with decreased likelihood of reporting any anxiety disorders in the past twelve months (OR = 0.2, p <0.05). Religious attendance of less than once/week, compared to attendance one or more times/week, was also significantly associated with decreased likelihood of reporting any 12-month anxiety disorders (OR = 0.6, p <0.05). Compared with respondents with a $35,000—$74,999 household income, those with less than $15,000 showed decreased likelihood of reporting any 12-month anxiety disorders (OR = 0.6, p <.05). Although the specific contrast between IUSC Other Latinos and IUSC Mexicans was significant in the Final Model as noted above, the effect was not large enough to make the omnibus test at the bottom of Table 3 significant. Indeed, none of the three omnibus tests for the Final Model were significant.

SUBSTANCE USE DISORDERS

Prevalence of 12-month substance use disorders were estimated to be literally zero among those persons aged 65 years or older in the sample (N = 228), and

TABLE 3

Logistic regression models for 12-month depressive, anxiety, and substance disorders

	12-month depressive disorders		12-month anxiety disorders		12-month substance disorders[a]	
	Model 1 (N = 2,546)	Final Model (N = 2,112)	Model 1 (N = 2,546)	Final Model (N = 2,112)	Model 1 (N = 1,825)	Final Model (N = 1,479)
Subethnicity by nativity subgroups						
Mexican in US as child	1.00	1.00	1.00	1.00	1.00	1.00
Puerto Rican in US as child	0.92 [0.59, 1.44]	0.71 [0.41, 1.22]	1.55 [0.94, 2.57]	1.03 [0.57, 1.87]	1.12 [0.52, 2.42]	0.53 [0.15, 1.97]
Cuban in US as child	0.42 [0.19, 0.90]*	0.44 [0.12, 1.63]	0.96 [0.43, 2.15]	0.93 [0.30, 2.92]	0.93 [0.36, 2.43]	2.87 [0.62, 13.22]
Other Latino in US as child	0.78 [0.44, 1.39]	0.61 [0.28, 1.33]	0.51 [0.23, 1.14]	0.42 [0.18, 0.97]*	1.17 [0.58, 2.36]	1.69 [0.46, 6.23]
Mexican later arrival immigrant	0.54 [0.38, 0.76]***	0.72 [0.28, 1.87]	0.63 [0.34, 1.18]	1.07 [0.35, 3.32]	0.35 [0.10, 1.30]	0.54 [0.15, 1.94]
Puerto Rican later arrival migrant	1.57 [0.92, 2.65]	1.59 [0.70, 3.62]	1.29 [0.68, 2.43]	1.43 [0.68, 2.99]	0.23 [0.03, 2.00]	0.22 [0.01, 3.26]
Cuban later arrival immigrant	0.88 [0.57, 1.36]	1.33 [0.67, 2.63]	1.09 [0.71, 1.68]	1.97 [0.85, 4.57]	0.55 [0.16, 1.92]	0.89 [0.11, 6.89]
Other Latino later arrival immigrant	0.78 [0.50, 1.21]	0.97 [0.45, 2.11]	0.78 [0.49, 1.26]	1.08 [0.47, 2.50]	0.33 [0.07, 1.53]	0.58 [0.07, 5.06]
Derived estimates:						
Later arrival immigrant vs. in US as child						
Mexican later arrival immigrant vs. in US as child	0.54 [0.38, 0.76]***	0.72 [0.28, 1.87]	0.63 [0.34, 1.18]	1.07 [0.35, 3.32]	0.35 [0.10, 1.30]	0.54 [0.15, 1.94]
Puerto Rican later arrival immigrant vs. in US as child	1.70 [0.95, 3.06]	2.23 [0.96, 5.22]	0.83 [0.47, 1.48]	1.39 [0.69, 2.81]	0.20 [0.02, 1.73]	0.41 [0.03, 4.75]
Cuban later arrival immigrant vs. in US as child	2.12 [0.97, 4.63]	2.99 [0.78, 11.44]	1.14 [0.54, 2.41]	2.11 [0.69, 6.46]	0.59 [0.12, 2.86]	0.31 [0.04, 2.39]
Other Latino later arrival immigrant vs. in US as child	1.00 [0.60, 1.67]	1.58 [0.69, 3.61]	1.54 [0.74, 3.18]	2.55 [0.92, 7.10]	0.28 [0.05, 1.56]	0.34 [0.02, 7.57]
Gender and age						
Female	1.73 [1.28, 2.33]***	1.43 [0.86, 2.40]	1.65 [1.13, 2.41]*	1.52 [0.91, 2.52]	0.26 [0.12, 0.52]***	0.12 [0.04, 0.36]***

Age (y)						
18–24	0.79 [0.39, 1.61]	0.59 [0.27, 1.30]	1.20 [0.80, 1.82]	0.74 [0.46, 1.21]	1.08 [0.40, 2.90]	0.43 [0.14, 1.31]
25–34	1.00	1.00	1.00	1.00	1.00	1.00
35–49	0.79 [0.49, 1.25]	0.80 [0.49, 1.31]	1.08 [0.76, 1.55]	1.34 [0.84, 2.16]	1.12 [0.59, 2.15]	1.37 [0.66, 2.86]
50–64	0.69 [0.43, 1.12]	0.70 [0.37, 1.30]	1.20 [0.82, 1.76]	1.61 [0.99, 2.63]	0.78 [0.14, 4.42]	1.25 [0.20, 7.96]
≥65	0.89 [0.44, 1.74]	0.89 [0.36, 2.18]	0.69 [0.26, 1.85]	0.64 [0.20, 2.01]	0.78 [0.14, 4.42]	1.25 [0.20, 7.96]
Immigration factors						
One or both parents US born vs. average in US as child	1.21 [0.92, 1.58]			1.28 [0.97, 1.68]		1.34 [0.83, 2.17]
Both parents foreign born vs. average in US as child	0.63 [0.36, 1.13]			0.56 [0.34, 0.92]*		0.76 [0.42, 1.40]
0–6 vs. average in US as child	1.17 [0.50, 2.72]			1.23 [0.79, 1.90]		0.52 [0.08, 3.17]
7–17 vs. average later arrival immigrant	1.10 [0.70, 1.72]			0.84 [0.58, 1.21]		0.80 [0.27, 2.39]
18–24 vs. average later arrival immigrant	1.00 [0.62, 1.62]			1.05 [0.76, 1.43]		1.22 [0.45, 3.33]
≥25 vs. average later arrival immigrant	0.92 [0.62, 1.36]			1.13 [0.81, 1.57]		
Acculturation factor						
English language proficiency						
Excellent or good	1.30 [0.58, 2.90]			1.47 [0.63, 3.43]		1.58 [0.44, 5.75]
Fair or poor	1.00			1.00		1.00
Enculturation factors						
Spanish language proficiency						
Excellent or good	1.13 [0.61, 2.08]			1.32 [0.85, 2.05]		1.03 [0.35, 3.04]
Fair or poor	1.00			1.00		1.00
Latino ethnic identity scale	0.53 [0.21, 1.37]			0.49 [0.16, 1.49]		2.14 [0.62, 7.38]
Family stressors and social supports						
Family support scale	0.60 [0.31, 1.18]			0.44 [0.18, 1.04]		0.91 [0.26, 3.22]
Family burden scale	3.03 [1.25, 7.35]*			6.02 [2.39, 15.12]***		3.03 [0.68, 13.57]

continued

TABLE 3 (Continued)
Logistic regression models for 12-month depressive, anxiety, and substance disorders

	12-month depressive disorders		12-month anxiety disorders		12-month substance disorders[a]	
	Model 1 (N = 2,546)	Final Model (N = 2,112)	Model 1 (N = 2,546)	Final Model (N = 2,112)	Model 1 (N = 1,825)	Final Model (N = 1,479)
Family cultural conflict scale		2.66 [1.31, 5.40]**		3.20 [1.56, 6.56]**		3.18 [0.76, 13.28]
Religious attendance						
≥1 per week		1.00		1.00		1.00
<1 per week		0.85 [0.46, 1.60]		0.63 [0.42, 0.95]*		1.32 [0.50, 3.49]
Never		0.98 [0.60, 1.59]		1.14 [0.71, 1.83]		3.46 [1.55, 7.72]**
Contextual factors						
Neighborhood safety scale		0.29 [0.13, 0.62]**		0.54 [0.20, 1.46]		0.008 [0.02, 0.33]**
Discrimination scale		3.03 [0.86, 10.62]		4.94 [1.35, 18.02]*		4.00 [0.91, 17.60]
Social status factors						
Marital status						
Married		1.00		1.00		1.00
Divorced, separated, widowed		2.04 [1.45, 2.89]***		1.15 [0.73, 1.82]		0.47 [0.14, 1.55]
Never married		1.56 [0.94, 2.59]		1.58 [1.03, 2.44]*		2.39 [1.28, 4.47]**
Employment status						
Employed		1.00		1.00		1.00
Unemployed		0.93 [0.36, 2.44]		1.40 [0.88, 2.23]		0.82 [0.20, 3.42]
Out of work force		1.78 [1.17, 2.73]		2.69 [1.62, 4.45]***		2.13 [0.80, 5.62]

42

Education (y)				
No high school (<9)		1.11 [0.68, 1.81]	0.71 [0.36, 1.40]	0.92 [0.36, 2.38]
Some high school (9–11)		0.91 [0.45, 1.84]	0.76 [0.42, 1.37]	1.29 [0.58, 2.88]
High school graduate (12)		1.00	1.00	1.00
Some college (13–15)		1.09 [0.54, 2.18]	0.69 [0.38, 1.26]	1.11 [0.49, 2.50]
College degree or greater (≥16)		1.76 [0.92, 3.38]	0.55 [0.24, 1.26]	0.76 [0.17, 3.39]
Household income ($)				
0–14,999		1.04 [0.61, 1.79]	0.59 [0.35, 0.99]*	0.67 [0.20, 2.25]
15,000–34,999		0.75 [0.39, 1.45]	0.93 [0.55, 1.57]	1.13 [0.32, 3.96]
35,000–74,999		1.00	1.00	1.00
≥75,000		0.98 [0.46, 2.09]	1.29 [0.73, 2.28]	0.72 [0.13, 4.02]
Perceived social standing in US community scale		0.24 [0.07, 0.78]*	0.23 [0.07, 0.71]*	0.27 [0.08, 0.92]*
Tests				
Differences among eight subethnicity by nativity groups (7 df)	**	NS	NS	NS
Later arrival immigrant vs. in US as child, stratified by subethnicity (4 df)	*	NS	NS	*
Interaction of nativity by subethnicity (3 df)	**	NS	NS	NS

NS, nonsignificant ($p \geq 0.05$). *$p <0.05$, **$p <0.01$ ***$p < 0.001$.
[a]Restricted to respondents ≤65 years of age.

were near zero (only one person observed with 12-month substance disorder) among immigrants whose age at arrival was 25 years or older ($N = 640$). Analysis of substance use disorders in Table 3 was thus restricted to the subsample (78% of total weighted sample; $N = 1,825$) of persons younger than age 65, excluding immigrants whose age of arrival was 25 years or older. In Model 1 (with age and gender adjustments), the omnibus test of differences between LAI and IUSC Latinos across the four subethnic groups was significant for 12-month substance use disorders ($p < 0.05$), with all groups showing a protective effect for LAIs, when contrasted to IUSCs. However, none of the individual odds ratios were significantly different from IUSC Mexicans, probably due to the small sample size. As anticipated, once we adjust for immigration, acculturation, and enculturation factors, as well as family, contextual, and social status variables in the Final Model, the omnibus test for comparing LAI and IUSC Latinos is no longer significant. In the Final Model, female gender (OR = 0.1, $p < 0.001$) and perceived neighborhood safety (OR = 0.1, $p < 0.01$) appear as protective factors, while never attending religious services compared to attending more than once a week (OR = 3.5, $p < 0.01$), and never being married compared to being married (OR = 2.4, $p < 0.01$) appear as risk factors for substance use disorders. Once again, as with the findings for both depressive and anxiety disorders, self-perceived high social standing in the US community is significantly associated with decreased likelihood of reporting any substance use disorder in the past twelve months (OR = 0.3, $p < 0.05$).

DISCUSSION

Consistent with previous findings (Grant et al. 2004), Mexican immigrants who arrive after age 6 to the US show lower risk of depressive disorders than their IUSC counterparts, after age and gender adjustments. As reported in past studies (Escobedo, Kirch, and Anda 1996; Narrow, Rae, Moscicki, Locke, and Regier 1990), IUSC Cubans also reported significantly lower prevalence of depressive disorders than IUSC Mexicans, showing that the risk for US-born Latinos might differ across subethnic groups. Less perceived discrimination, greater neighborhood safety, and lower family conflict and burden appear to contribute to decreased prevalence of depressive disorders among IUSC Cubans in comparison to IUSC Mexicans. Once we adjust for these contextual and family differences in the Final Model, the differences in risk become insignificant.

In contrast, the eight ethnicity/nativity subgroups are not significantly different for anxiety after adjusting for age and gender. It seems that Other Latinos (mostly Bolivians, Nicaraguans, Salvadorians and Colombians) who arrived in the US as children had lower risk of anxiety disorders compared to IUSC Mexicans, after adjusting for all other factors. However, this contrast was not predicted and it was not strong enough to yield a significant omnibus test, which was designed to control Type I error. We note this difference so that it can be monitored in future studies.

As hypothesized, family burden and family cultural conflict, perceived low neighborhood safety, exposure to discrimination, disrupted marital status, being out of the labor force, and perceived low social standing all to varying degrees figure as risk factors for 12-month depressive, anxiety, and substance use disorders (as shown in the Final Models of Table 3). This implies that demonstrated differences in prevalence of psychiatric disorders among Latinos by ethnicity/nativity subgroups are a function of multiple factors beyond foreign nativity. These results help explain the inconsistent findings of other studies regarding whether foreign nativity is protective against psychiatric disorders, given that type of disorder and variables included in adjustments might produce different results across studies.

We identified several risk and protective factors linked to psychiatric disorders as Latinos integrate into US society. Elevated family cultural conflict and family burden are associated with increased risk for depressive and anxiety disorders. This is consistent with Hovey's findings (2000a, b) showing that family dysfunction and ineffective social support predict depression. After adjusting for family cultural conflict and family burden, LAI Mexicans experience similar risk for depressive disorders as IUSC Mexicans, suggesting the importance of family harmony to counter depression. These factors remain significant, even after adjusting for differences in marital status, perceived neighborhood safety, or social status.

We found no differences in risk for anxiety disorders for LAI relative to IUSC Latinos after age and sex adjustments. Our findings question the existence of a protective effect of nativity for past-year anxiety disorders. Nonetheless, foreign parental nativity emerges as a protective factor for anxiety disorders for US-born Latinos (i.e., after adjusting for the LAI/IUSC distinction). Foreign parental nativity may inhibit the internalization of US-society lifestyles, including expectations that might be incongruous with one's perceived social status (Dressler 1988), diminishing the risk for anxiety disorders. For example, US expectations for the disadvantaged may be unrealistic, with pressure to succeed and achieve the "American dream" without the opportunities to do so (Hochschild 1995). Expectations for those whose parents were foreign-born (e.g., having healthy children, getting married) may be more compatible with the hardships and struggles of the disadvantaged, providing for a less stressful and disempowering experience of everyday life, and consequently lower risk for anxiety disorders. These findings highlight the importance of intergenerational effects on health outcomes.

One surprising result from our analysis is that low income (family income less than $15,000) seems to be associated with less anxiety disorder relative to higher income ($35,000—$74,999). This seems to fly in the face of considerable literature on economic disadvantage. In sensitivity analyses, we determined that this association only appeared when we adjusted for perceived social standing. This suggests that higher perceived social standing may suppress the potentially negative effect of low income, given that once we removed social standing from the model in sensitivity analyses, the protective effect of low income for anxiety disorders is no longer observed. We also cannot rule out that for Latinos in poverty, limited expectations for social mobility might provide a buffer from the stresses of low income and be protective for anxiety disorders (Breslau et al. 2006).

After age and gender adjustments (Model 1), LAI have lower risk for 12-month substance use disorders, independent of subethnicity, when contrasted to IUSC Latinos. This supports the persistence of the Latino immigrant paradox in substance use disorders. Perceived level of neighborhood safety also seems associated with lower risk for substance use disorders. This finding is consistent with other research (Cho, Park, and Echevarria-Cruz 2005; Lambert, Brown, Phillips, and Ialongo 2004; Wandersman and Nation 1998) which emphasizes the importance of the receiving context, particularly early exposure to neighborhood disadvantage as a risk factor for illness, even after controlling for individual-level socioeconomic status. For substance use disorders, the importance of arrival to the US after age 25 offers insight into the context-dependent risk for substance use disorders. Coming to the US as an adult might protect against exposure to risky social networks linked to drug use. Religious attendance also emerges as a factor that facilitates social participation and integration into positive social networks that protect against the negative impact of disadvantageous neighborhoods. This is consistent with evidence that religious involvement may be a protective factor against substance disorders (Miller 1998), with the church functioning as a source of social control that discourages deviance.

There are certain limitations of this study. Most importantly, although a cross-sectional study helps us understand some aspects of the process of acculturation and enculturation, identifying causality is best assessed using a longitudinal approach. Some of the observed associations could reflect reverse causation, such as the possibility that family conflict is an outcome of depressive or anxiety disorders. Another limitation involves disentangling the effect of variables that are only proxies for certain cultural processes. For example, while Spanish proficiency might relate to internalization of Latino cultural values and attitudes, it does not indicate which values and attitudes might be protective. Language could also reflect the presence of different networks and lifestyles, independent of acculturation. However, these findings do suggest important future directions for research, such as the importance of contextual environment, religious attendance, and perceived social status for substance-use disorders. For example, findings presented in Table 2 suggest that LAI Latinos with significantly lower incomes live in neighborhoods they perceive to be less safe and report lower social standing in their US communities, increasing the importance of context in the prospective risk for psychiatric illness.

Our findings show that nativity may be a less important independent risk factor for current psychiatric morbidity than originally thought. In other words, it is not nativity per se that protects from psychiatric illness once immigrants arrive in the US, but rather family, contextual, and social status factors associated with nativity and age of arrival in the US. Family harmony, marital status, integration in employment and self-perception of high social standing appear to be central to decreased risk of depressive and anxiety disorders for Latinos in the US, while late arrival, perceived neighborhood safety, religious attendance, and self-perceptions of high social standing appear more relevant as protective factors for substance-use disorders. The within-group variation among Latinos means that ethnicity/nativity subcategories mask meaningful differences in historic and current living circumstances of ethnic minority populations.

Our results question the generalizability of the finding that all Latino immigrants have better mental health than US-born Latinos. Among Mexicans, once we adjust for family factors, we find no differences between IUSC and LAI. A more complicated picture emerges whereby the risk of psychiatric disorders, depending on the disorder, can be a function of family burden and family conflict, as well as the availability of effective family supports, the contextual environment (including exposure to discrimination, perceived neighborhood safety, and religious attendance) and self-perceived social status in the US. Most studies of the "immigrant paradox" lack explanatory factors specific to the Latino experience, and ignore the challenges of disentangling effects of nativity from other risk factors. Our findings suggest that comparing groups of Latinos by subethnicity and nativity is an important way to sort out potential mechanisms involved in increasing or decreasing risk of psychiatric disorders for Latinos living in the United States.

ACKNOWLEDGMENT

The NLAAS data used in this analysis was provided by the Center for Multicultural Mental Health Research at the Cambridge Health Alliance. The project was supported by NIH Research Grant # U01 MH62209 funded by the National Institute of Mental Health as well as the Substance Abuse and Mental Health Services Administration/Center for Mental Health Services and the Office of Behavioral and Social Science Research. This publication was also made possible by Grant #P20 MD000537 from the National Center on Minority Health and Health Disparities (NCMHD) and Grant #P50 MH07346902 from the National Institute of Mental Health.

REFERENCES

Adler, N., E. Epel, G. Castellazzo, and J. Ickovics. 2000. Relationship of subjective and objective social status with psychological and physiological functioning: Preliminary data in healthy white women. *Health Psychology* 19(6):586–92.

Alegría, M., R. Bijl, E. Lin, E. Walters, and R. Kessler. 2000. Income differences in persons seeking outpatient treatment for mental disorders: A comparison of the United States with Ontario and the Netherlands: A comparison of the United States with Ontario and the Netherlands. *Archives of General Psychiatry* 57(4):383–91.

Alegría, M., G. Canino, F. Stinson, and B. Grant. 2006. Nativity and DSM-IV psychiatric disorders among Puerto Ricans, Cuban Americans and non-Latino Whites in the United States: Results from the National Epidemiologic Survey on Alcohol and Related Conditions. *Journal of Clinical Psychiatry* 67(1):56–65.

Alegría, M., N. Mulvaney-Day, M. Torres, A. Polo, Z. Cao, and G. Canino. 2007. Prevalence of psychiatric disorders across Latino subgroups in the United States. *American Journal of Public Health* 97:68–75.

Alegría, M., D. Takeuchi, G. Canino, N. Duan, P. Shrout, X.-L. Meng, et al. 2004. Considering context, place and culture: The National Latino and Asian American Study. *International Journal of Methods in Psychiatric Research* 13(4):208–20.

Alegría, M., D. Vila, M. Woo, G. Canino, D. Takeuchi, M. Vera, et al. 2004. Cultural relevance and equivalence in the NLAAS instrument: Integrating Etic and Emic in the development of cross-cultural measures for a psychiatric epidemiology and services study of Latinos. *International Journal of Methods in Psychiatric Research* 13(4):270–88.

Anderson, M., and S. Fienberg. 1999. *Who counts?: The politics of census-taking in contemporary America.* New York: Russell Sage Foundation.

Blank, S., and R. Torrechila. 1998. Understanding the living arrangements of Latino immigrants: A life course approach. *International Migration Review* 32(1):3–19.

Boswell, T. 2002. *A demographic profile of Cuban Americans*: The Cuban American National Council.

Breslau, J., S. Aguilar-Gaxiola, K. S. Kendler, M. Su, D. Williams, and R. Kessler. 2006. Specifying race-ethnic differences in risk for psychiatric disorder in a USA national sample. *Psychological Medicine* 36(1):57–68.

Burnam, M. A., R. Hough, M. Karno, J. Escobar, and C. Telles. 1987. Acculturation and lifetime prevalence of psychiatric disorders among Mexican Americans in Los Angeles. *Journal of Health and Social Behavior* 28:89–102.

Capps, R., M. Fix, J. Ost, J. Reardon-Anderson, and J. Passel. 2004. *The health and well-being of young children of immigrants.* Urban Institute.

Cho, Y., G.-S. Park, and S. Echevarria-Cruz. 2005. Perceived neighborhood characteristics and the health of adult Koreans. *Social Science and Medicine* 60(6):1285–97.

Cortes, D., R. Malgady, and L. Rogler. 1994. Biculturality among Puerto Rican adults in the United States. *American Journal of Community Psychology* 22(5):707–21.

Cortes, D. 1994. Acculturation and its relevance to mental health. In R. G. Malgady, and O. Rodriguez (Eds.), *Theoretical and conceptual issues in Hispanic mental health* (pp. 54–68). Melbourne, FL: Robert E. Krieger Publishing Co, Inc.

Dressler, W. 1988. Social consistency and psychological distress. *Journal of Health and Social Behavior* 29(1):79–91.

Escobar, J., C. H. Nervi, and M. Gara. 2000. Immigration and mental health: Mexican Americans in the United States. *Harvard Review of Psychiatry* 8(2):64–72.

Escobedo, L., D. Kirch, and R. Anda. 1996. Depression and smoking initiation among US Latinos. *Addiction* 91(1):113–19.

Felix-Ortiz, M., M. Newcomb, and H. Myers. 1994. A multidimensional measure of cultural identity for Latino and Latina adolescents. *Hispanic Journal of Behavioral Sciences* 16:99–115.

Finch, B., B. Kolody, and W. Vega. 2000. Perceived discrimination and depression among Mexican-origin adults in California. *Journal of Health and Social Behavior* 41:295–313.

Finch, B., and W. Vega. 2003. Acculturation stress, social support, and self-rated health among Latinos in California. *Journal of Immigrant Health* 5(3):109–17.

Grant, B., F. Stinson, D. Hasin, D. Dawson, P. Chou and K. Anderson. 2004. Immigration and lifetime prevalence of DSM-IV psychiatric disorders among Mexican Americans and non-Hispanic Whites in the United States. *Archives of General Psychiatry* 61(12):1226–1233.

Guarnaccia, P., I. Martinez, R. Ramirez, and G. Canino. 2005. Are ataques de nervios in Puerto Rican children associated with psychiatric disorder? *Journal of the American Academy of Child and Adolescent Psychiatry* 44(11):1184–92.

Guarnaccia, P., and O. Rodriguez. 1996. Concepts of culture and their role in the development of culturally competent mental health services. *Hispanic Journal of Behavioral Sciences* 18(4):419–41.

Hagan, J. 1998. Social networks, gender, and immigrant incorporation: Resources and constraints. *American Sociological Review* 63(1):55–67.

Heeringa, S., J. Wagner, M. Torres, N. Duan, T. Adams and P. Berglund. 2004. Sample designs and sampling methods for the collaborative psychiatric epidemiology studies CPES. *International Journal of Methods in Psychiatric Research* 13(4):221–40.

Hernandez, D., and E. Charney. 1998. *From generation to generation: The health and well-being of children in immigrant families.* Washington, DC: National Academy Press.

Hochschild, J. 1995. *Facing up to the American dream: Race, class, and the soul of the nation.* Princeton, NJ: Princeton University Press.

Hovey, J., and C. Magana. 2002. Cognitive, affective, and physiological expressions of anxiety symptomatology among Mexican migrant farmworkers: Predictors and generational differences. *Community Mental Health Journal* 38(3):223–37.

Hovey, J. 2000a. Acculturative stress, depression, and suicidal ideation among Central American immigrants. *Suicide and life-threatening behavior* 30(2):125–39.

Hovey, J. 2000b. Psychosocial predictors of depression among Central American immigrants. *Psychological Reports* 86:1237–40.

Jackson, J., M. Torres, C. Caldwell, H. Neighbors, R. Nesse, R. J. Taylor, et al. 2004. The national survey of American life: A study of racial, ethnic and cultural influences on mental disorders and mental health. *International Journal of Methods in Psychiatric Research* 13(4):196–207.

Jarvis, E., L. Kirmayer, M. Weinfeld, and J. Lasry. 2005. Religious practice and psychological distress: The importance of gender, ethnicity and immigrant status. *Transcultural Psychiatry* 42(4):657–75.

Kessler, R., and K. Merikangas. 2004. The national comorbidity survey-replication (NCS-R). *International Journal of Methods in Psychiatric Research* 13(2):60–68.

Kessler, R., and T. Ustun. 2004. The World mental health (WMH) survey initiative version of the World health organization (WHO) composite international diagnostic interview (CIDI). *International Journal of Methods in Psychiatric Research* 13(2):93–121.

Kim, B., and J. Abreu. 2001. Acculturation measurement: Theory, current instruments, and future directions. In G. Ponterotto, J. Casas, L. Suzuki, and C. Alexander (Eds.), *Handbook of multicultural counseling* (pp. 394–424). Thousand Oaks, CA: Sage.

Kim, B., and M. Ominzo. 2006. Behavioral acculturation and enculturation and psychological functioning among Asian American college students. *Cultural Diversity and Ethnic Minority Psychology* 12(2):245–58.

Klonoff, E., H. Landrine, and J. Ullman. 1999. Racial discrimination and psychiatric symptoms among Blacks. *Cultural Diversity and Ethnic Minority Psychology* 5(4):329–339.

LaFromboise, T., H. Coleman, and J. Gerton. 1993. Psychological impact of biculturalism: Evidence and theory. *Psychological Bulletin* 114(3):395–412.

Lambert, S., T. Brown, C. Phillips and N. Ialongo. 2004. The relationship between perceptions of neighborhood characteristics and substance use among Urban African American adolescents. *American Journal of Community Psychology* 34(3–4):205–19.

Lara, M., C. Gamboa, M. Kahramanian, L. Morales and D. Bautista. 2005. Acculturation and Latino health in the United States: A review of the literature and its sociopolitical context. *Annual Review of Public Health* 26:367–97.

Levitt, P. 1998. Local-level global religion: The case of US dominican migration. *Journal for the Scientific Study of Religion* 37(1):74–89.

Marin, B. V., and G. Marin. 1992. Predictors of condom accessibility among Hispanics in San Francisco. *American Journal of Public Health* 82(4):592–95.

Martinez, R., Jr. 1996. Latinos and lethal violence: The impact of poverty and inequality. *Social Problems* 43(2):131–46.

McKinlay, J., and L. Marceau. 1999. A tale of 3 tails. *American Journal of Public Health* 89(3):295–98.

Menjivar, C. 1999. Religious institutions and transnationalism: A case study of Catholic and Evangelical Salvadoran immigrants. *International Journal of Politics, Culture and Society* 12(4):589–612.

Miller, W. 1998. Researching the spiritual dimensions of alcohol and other drug problems. *Addiction* 93(7):979.

Narrow, W., D. Rae, E. Moscicki, B. Locke and D. Regier. 1990. Depression among Cuban Americans: The Hispanic health and nutrition examination survey. *Social Psychiatry and Psychiatric Epidemiology* 25:260–68.

Ortega, A., R. Rosenheck, M. Alegria and R. Desai. 2000. Acculturation and the lifetime risk of psychiatric and substance use disorders among Hispanics. *The Journal of Nervous and Mental Disease* 88(11):728–35.

Pellegrino, A. 2004. Migration from Latin America to Europe: Trends and policy challenges. International Organization on Migration.

Pennell, B., A. Bowers, D. Carr, S. Chardoul, G. Cheung, K. Dinkelmann, et al. 2004. The development and implementation of the national comorbidity survey replication, the national survey of American life, and the National Latino and Asian American survey. *International Journal of Methods in Psychiatric Research* 13(4):241–69.

Phillips, J. 2002. White, black, and Latino homicide rates: Why the difference? *Social Problems* 49(3):349–73.

Powers, M., and W. Seltzer. 1998. Occupational status and mobility among undocumented immigrants by gender. *International Migration Review* 32(1):21–55.

Rao, J., and A. Scott. 1984. On chi-squared tests for multiway contingency tables with cell proportions estimated from survey data. *Annals of Statistics* 12:46–60.

Rivera-Sinclair, E. 1997. Acculturation/biculturalism and it's relationship to adjustment in Cuban-Americans. *International Journal of Intercultural Relations* 21(3):379–91.

Rogler, L., D. Cortes and R. Malgady. 1991. Acculturation and mental health status among Hispanics: Convergence and new directions in research. *American Psychologist* 46:584–97.

Rumbaut, R. 2006. The making of a people. In The National Research Council (Ed.), *Hispanics and the Future of America*. Washington, DC: National Academies Press.

Singer, M., H. Baer, G. Scott, S. Horowitz and B. Weinstein. 1998. Pharmacy access to syringes among injecting drug users: Follow-up findings from Hartford, Connecticut. *Public Health Reports* 113(Suppl. 1):81–89.

Singh, G., and M. Siahpush. 2001. All-cause and cause-specific mortality of immigrants and native born in the United States. *American Journal of Public Health* 91(3):392–400.

Stata Corporation. 2004. *Stata statistical software release 8.2*. College Station, TX: Stata Corporation.

Suarez-Orozco, C., and M. Suarez-Orozco. 2001. *Children of immigration*. Cambridge, MA: Harvard University Press.

Suarez-Orozco, C., and I. Todorova. 2003. The social worlds of immigrant youth. *New Directions for Youth Development* 100(Winter):2, 15–24.

Sullivan, M., and R. Rehm. 2005. Mental health of undocumented Mexican immigrants: a review of the literature. *Advances in Nursing Science* 28(3):240–51.

Szalacha, L., S. Erkut, C. Garcia, O. Alarcon, J. Fields, and I. Ceder. 2003. Discrimination and Puerto Rican children's and adolescents' mental health. *Cultural Diversity and Ethnic Minority Psychology* 9:141–55.

US Census Bureau. 2000. *America's families and living arrangements*. Washington, DC: Current Population Reports.

Vega, W., B. Kolody, S. Aguilar-Gaxiola, E. Alderte, R. Catalano and H. Caraveo-Anduaga. 1998. Lifetime prevalence of DSM-III-R psychiatric disorders among urban and rural Mexican Americans in California. *Archives of General Psychiatry* 55(9):771–78.

Wallen, G., R. Feldman and J. Anliker. 2002. Measuring acculturation among Central American women with the use of a brief language scale. *Journal of Immigrant Health* 4(2):95–102.

Wandersman, A., and M. Nation. 1998. Urban neighborhoods and mental health. *American Psychologist* 53(6):647–56.

Williams, R. B., and C. Collins. 1995. US socioeconomic and racial differences in health: Patterns and explanations. *Annual Review of Sociology* 21:349–87.

Does Americanization Have Adverse Effects on Health?: Stress, Health Habits, and Infant Health Outcomes among Puerto Ricans

Nancy S. Landale, R. S. Oropesa,
Daniel Llánes, and
Bridget K. Gorman

The study of how immigrants to the US and their descendants become incorporated into American society has long been guided by assimilation theory (Gordon 1964; Park 1950; Park and Burgess 1921), which has recently reemerged as a topic of intense debate among scholars of ethnic relations. The classic assimilation perspective proposes that as immigrants spend time in the US they gradually replace their old cultural and behavioral patterns with those of the receiving society. Assimilation is generally conceived as a linear process that occurs across generations, with each new generation moving closer to complete cultural integration into the host society (Alba and Nee 1997). The assimilation perspective also suggests that the socioeconomic circumstances of immigrants improve with duration of residence and generational succession (Rumbaut 1997).[1]

The expectations of intergenerational improvement and gradual integration into the mainstream are at the heart of recent challenges to assimilation theory. A growing body of research on the adaptation of recent non-European immigrants demonstrates that some groups experience deteriorating circumstances across generations (Harris 1998; Landale, Oropesa and Gorman 1999; Oropesa and Landale 1997; Rumbaut 1997; Zhou 1997). This unexpected pat-

Nancy S. Landale, R.S. Oropesa, Daniel Llánes, and Bridget K. Gorman: "Does Americanization Have Adverse Effects on Health? Street, Health Habits, and Infant Health Outcomes among Puerto Ricans," from *Social Forces*, Volume 78, no. 2 (December 1999): 613–41.

tern in outcomes ranging from family structure to academic achievement is interpreted by some scholars as evidence that the assimilation process is variable. For some immigrant groups, assimilation into the middle-class majority proceeds in a roughly linear fashion. However, others appear to assimilate into the disadvantaged segments of society. For these groups, assimilation may result in negative outcomes (Zhou 1997).

Although most sociological studies of the assimilation process focus on socioeconomic outcomes, several health outcomes also exhibit patterns that are at odds with the classic assimilation model. For example, a growing body of research demonstrates that impoverished immigrant groups, especially Mexicans and Southeast Asians, have infant health outcomes that are better than expected on the basis of their socioeconomic profiles. Conventional theories of assimilation imply that such groups should exhibit worse outcomes than non-Latino whites, but both Mexican and Southeast Asian immigrants have lower rates of low birth weight and infant mortality than the non-Latino white population (Rumbaut and Weeks 1989; Williams, Binken and Clingman 1986). Further, generational comparisons within the Mexican-origin population show that pregnancy outcomes are substantially better for foreign-born women than for native-born women (Collins and Shay 1994; Guendelman 1995).[2] This epidemiological paradox further demonstrates that Americanization is not always beneficial for immigrant groups.

Despite the strength of the evidence demonstrating the existence of the epidemiological paradox, the social processes underlying generational differences in birth outcomes remain poorly understood. Most explanations emphasize the influence of assimilation on women's lifestyles, broadly defined, but empirical studies focus exclusively on the role of a few specific health behaviors (e.g., smoking) owing to a paucity of data on other aspects of pregnant women's everyday lives. Nonetheless, there is growing interest in ascertaining the mechanisms through which assimilation influences reproductive health outcomes. To do so requires in-depth study of how the situations and health habits of pregnant women differ across generations of US residents. It also requires expanding the focus of inquiry to include ethnic groups other than the Mexican-origin population.

In this article, we use recently collected data from the Puerto Rican Maternal and Infant Health Study to examine the social circumstances and health behaviors of pregnant Puerto Rican women living in the continental US Puerto Ricans are an important ethnic group to examine because they are the second-largest Latino group in the US and one of the three US minority groups with the poorest infant health outcomes.[3] They are also a group with a high and persistent rate of poverty, which some have argued is so chronic that they should be considered part of the "underclass" (Lemann 1991).

Our analysis focuses on generational differences in stressful life events and health habits during pregnancy and on the implications of those differences for infant health outcomes. Overall, our results show that US-born Puerto Rican women experience a greater number of stressful life events and engage in more negative health behaviors during pregnancy than Puerto Rican-born migrants to the US mainland. However, it is only relatively recent migrants who exhibit an advantage with respect to the health of their offspring.

THEORETICAL BACKGROUND

SEGMENTED ASSIMILATION

What are the factors that lead some immigrant groups to experience rapid assimilation into the middle-class mainstream and others to experience deteriorating outcomes as they spend more time in the US? Explanations of the diverse pathways of assimilation focus largely on how risk and protective factors change with duration of residence and generational status (Portes and Zhou 1993). Major risk factors for generational decline include a constellation of circumstances related to poverty: low levels of financial and human capital, limited opportunities for economic advancement, residence in disadvantaged neighborhoods, and high levels of exposure to stressful life events. The negative consequences of these conditions can be attenuated by protective factors, the most notable of which are the cultural assets and social support networks of immigrant groups.

A fundamental determinant of the assimilation pathway taken by an immigrant group is the level of resources available to its members at the time of arrival. Clearly, it is critical to distinguish between highly educated immigrants who come to the US for professional job opportunities and immigrants with little education and technical expertise who come seeking manual labor. The human and financial capital possessed by the former groups allows them to integrate quickly into middle-class society because they have the skills to obtain high-level professional and technical jobs and the funds to move directly into middle-class suburban neighborhoods. In contrast, groups with less education and fewer financial resources start at the bottom of the occupational hierarchy. The fate of such immigrants is largely determined by opportunities for economic advancement, which in recent years have become increasingly scarce for workers with little education and skill (Zhou 1997).

Intergenerational changes in expectations and attitudes also play a role in the assimilation process. Some scholars (Portes and Zhou 1993) argue that the reference group for expectations shifts from the country of origin for the first generation to the native-born majority for the second.[4] As a consequence of their higher expectations, the second generation is more aware of discrimination and barriers to mobility than the first (Kaplan and Marks 1990). The concentration of impoverished immigrant groups in central-city areas further contributes to generational differences in outlook. Although both the first and the second generations are in contact with disadvantaged native-born minorities because of their residence in the central city, the second generation is less insulated from inner-city street life and the subcultures of native-born minority groups because its interactions are less confined to the family and the ethnic community. As a result, the US-born children of immigrants are more likely to adopt the attitudes and behaviors of native-born minority youth. In short, because of shared circumstances and residential propinquity, the second generation may become increasingly similar to native-born minorities rather than to the middle-class majority.

These various risk factors for negative assimilation are prominent among Puerto Rican migrants to the US In-migrants from Puerto Rico have relatively low educational attainment (Bean and Tienda 1987; Rivera-Batiz and Santiago 1996) and limited economic resources, which has resulted in their concentration in inner-city neighborhoods of large northeastern cities, principally New York. Among Latinos, Puerto Ricans occupy a uniquely disadvantaged position. They have a lower rate of labor force participation, a higher rate of unemployment, and a substantially higher poverty rate than the other major US Latino subgroups (Bean and Tienda 1987; Sandefur and Tienda 1988; Torres and Rodriguez 1991). Although a turnaround in the trend of declining economic well-being that was documented for Puerto Ricans during the 1970s has occurred in recent years, a significant share of the mainland Puerto Rican population is stuck on the bottom rungs of the income ladder (Torres and Rodriguez 1991). Thus, some have argued that Puerto Ricans have become part of the "urban underclass."[5]

Persistent Disadvantage, Stress, and Maternal Health Behaviors

Chronic poverty and residence in distressed central-city neighborhoods increase the probability of exposure to acute and chronic stressors that have negative repercussions for physical and mental health (Krieger et al. 1993). For example, disadvantaged minority women have greater exposure to crime, environmental pollutants, inadequate housing, family instability, and destructive health habits (e.g., substance abuse) than others. Gans (1992) argues that negative assimilation may increase the likelihood of experiencing such stressful conditions: "One likely result of second-generation decline is higher unemployment among that generation; another is the possibility of more crime, alcoholism, drug use, as well as increases in the other pathologies that go with poverty—and with the frustration of rising expectations" (183).

The role of such stressful conditions in maternal and infant health is not yet fully understood. After reviewing the results of epidemiological studies of various populations, McLean et al. (1993) conclude that there is cumulative support for the hypothesis that high levels of exposure to stressors contribute to poor birth outcomes, especially low birth weight and preterm delivery. Yet the mechanisms through which stressful life events affect reproductive outcomes have not been specified. Possible mechanisms include changes in neuroendocrine functioning, immune system responses, and adverse habits such as smoking and drug use (Chomitz, Cheung and Lieberman 1995). The extent to which the consequences of stress for birth outcomes can be modified by financial and social assets is also unclear (but see Aneshensel 1992 for a general discussion of the stress-buffering effects of resources).

Implications For Nativity Differences In Lifestyle And Infant Health

Both segmented assimilation theory and empirical studies documenting the epidemiological paradox indicate that the assimilation process does not invariably lead to improvements in health and well-being. The above-mentioned studies of links between persistent disadvantage, stressful life events, and birth outcomes suggest one process through which the broader structural

position of an immigrant group may affect infant health. Although studies of
the epidemiological paradox have not attempted to place their findings within
the context of broader theoretical debates about the nature of the assimilation process, they have emphasized intergenerational changes in lifestyle factors. Nativity differentials have been documented in habits such as smoking,
drinking, drug use, and nutritional intake (Guendelman 1995; Guendelman
and Abrams 1995; Guendelman and English 1995; Landale, Oropesa and Gorman 1999; Zambrana et al. 1997). For example, using data from the Linked
Birth-Infant Death Data Sets[6] for the 1989–91 birth cohorts, Landale, Oropesa,
and Gorman (1999) show that foreign-born women are less likely to smoke
during pregnancy than native-born women in each of 10 ethnic groups examined. Similar patterns have been found for drinking and drug use (Guendelman 1995), and limited evidence suggests that nutritional intake also worsens
with time in the US (Guendelman and Abrams 1995).

Potential explanations of these patterns are (1) greater exposure to stressors, which may be objective (e.g., chronic poverty, high levels of neighborhood
disorganization) or subjective (e.g., perceived discrimination, unmet expectations) in nature, and (2) a loss of protective influences, especially origin-coun-
try cultural norms and networks of social support. Explanations that focus
on the erosion of protective factors typically emphasize the greater familism
of immigrants compared to nonimmigrants (Kaplan and Marks 1990). For
example, traditional Latino cultures emphasize the needs of the family over
those of the individual. Motherhood is highly regarded and viewed as wom-
en's most important role (Fennelly 1992). Moreover, Latinos are reported to
have closer kin networks than non-Latinos. Close kin networks may provide
information about pregnancy and resources available to pregnant women,
encourage healthy behaviors during pregnancy, and reduce stress by providing psychological support (Guendelman 1995). Assimilation may lower the
value placed on motherhood and weaken the family ties that support mothers
and their children (Oropesa and Gorman 1998). In general, the protective role
of the family has been emphasized in studies that find better infant health
outcomes for the foreign-born than the native-born, even though the foreign-
born have a poorer objective position.

RESEARCH QUESTIONS

In the following analysis, we examine the implications of the migration and
assimilation processes for the lifestyles and health habits of pregnant Puerto
Rican women. We determine the extent to which there are differences by generational status in Puerto Rican women's exposure to stressful life events and
their substance-use patterns during pregnancy. In addition, we assess the
roles of lifestyle and health habits in explaining generational differences in
two key indicators of infant health—low birth weight and infant mortality.

Our study advances prior research in several important ways. First, we
focus on a population that has received little attention in studies of assimilation and infant health. Research to date has emphasized the Mexican-origin
population. Understanding the effects of migration on maternal and infant

health requires study of the circumstances and outcomes of a variety of migratory groups. Second, many prior studies of the issues addressed in this article suffer from data limitations. Specifically, those based on nationally representative data (e.g., vital records) typically lack adequate information on women's lifestyles and on key explanatory variables. More detailed information is often available from smaller samples (e.g., clinic-based samples), but such samples are rarely representative of the larger population of concern. As discussed below, the data used in this study come from a representative sample of Puerto Rican mothers from the six US states with the greatest number of births to Puerto Rican women. The sample was drawn from the vital records, but detailed information was collected from the mothers through in-person interviews to supplement the vital records data.

The interview data allow us to examine a variety of indicators of women's lifestyles during pregnancy, each of which potentially affects the health of the pregnant woman and her offspring. In addition, accurate information on infant birth weight and survival was obtained from the vital records. Because our data include a wide range of explanatory variables, we provide a more complete test of explanations of generational decline in health-related lifestyle factors than previous research. Explanations of negative assimilation identify low human capital, meager financial resources, and residence in disadvantaged neighborhoods as factors that increase the risk of deteriorating outcomes across generations. In addition, the loss of protective influences, such as strong family support and a Latino cultural orientation, may contribute to generational decline. We assess whether generational differences in exposure to stressful life events, health habits, and birth outcomes can be explained in terms of resources (e.g., financial and social) and cultural orientation. Arguments about the causes of generational decline also emphasize the contexts in which groups reside. In addition to our tests of individual-level explanations, we assess the role of neighborhood characteristics in contributing to generational patterns in pregnant women's lifestyles and the health of their offspring.

DATA AND MEASURES

Data and Study Population

The analysis is based on data from the Puerto Rican Maternal and Infant Health Study (PRMIHS), a study of maternal and infant health outcomes among Puerto Ricans in the US and Puerto Rico.[7] In-person interviews were conducted with 2,631 mothers of infants sampled from the 1994 and 1995 birth and infant death records of six US states (Connecticut, Florida, Massachusetts, New Jersey, New York, Pennsylvania) and the Commonwealth of Puerto Rico.[8] Infants were eligible for inclusion in the birth sample if the Hispanic ethnicity of the mother was designated as Puerto Rican on the birth certificate. Infants who died before their first birthday were eligible for inclusion in the death sample if they were identified as Puerto Rican on the death certificate or if their mother was classified as Puerto Rican on the birth certificate. Roughly two-thirds of the interviews (1,863) were with mothers of infants sampled from the computerized birth certificate files maintained by the states and Puerto Rico. The remaining 768 interviews were with mothers of infants drawn from death certificates for infant deaths.

The study design called for locating the mothers of the sampled infants from the address information provided on the vital records and requesting their participation in a computer-assisted personal interview (CAPI). All study interviewers were bilingual, and the questionnaire was available in both Spanish and English. Response rates for the birth and death samples, respectively, were 79% and 74%.

The present study is based primarily on the birth sample, which can be considered representative of 1994–95 births to Puerto Rican women residing in the study area.[9] By extension, the birth sample represents Puerto Rican mothers of infants born in the specified area and period of time. A limitation of representative samples of births, however, is that there are typically too few cases of infant death to allow for the study of infant mortality. To overcome this limitation, the PRMIHS included all death cases in the study area during the designated time frame. We use this oversample of infant death cases in our analysis of infant mortality.

Our analyses are restricted to mothers of US-born infants because we are concerned with the experiences of Puerto Rican women living in the mainland US In addition, we eliminate cases in which the respondent was born outside the US and Puerto Rico and cases in which there were missing data on one or more of the predictors included in the analysis.[10] After these restrictions are made, our principal analytic sample consists of 1,146 mainland Puerto Rican mothers of infants born in 1994 and 1995.[11] Our analysis of infant mortality is based on data from 1,327 mothers because it includes the oversample of infant death cases drawn from the death certificates.

DEPENDENT VARIABLES

Our analysis of women's lifestyles while they were pregnant with the sampled infants focuses on three types of measures: (1) indicators of whether particular stressful life events occurred; (2) a subjective rating of stress; and (3) indicators of unhealthy behaviors, including smoking, drinking, and drug use. The questions on stressful life events asked the women whether they had experienced the following situations during the focal pregnancy:

1. Someone very close to you had a bad problem with drinking or drugs.
2. Your husband or partner went to jail.
3. You were homeless.
4. You lost your job even though you wanted to go on working.
5. You had a lot of bills you couldn't pay.
6. You were involved in a physical fight.
7. Your husband or partner hit you or physically hurt you.[12]

These stressful life events are analyzed as separate dichotomous variables and as an additive index with scores that range from 0 to 7. A separate question asked the women to describe the amount of stress they felt during the focal pregnancy. The response categories ranged from 0 to 4, with 0 indicating no stress and 4 denoting a very high level of distress. Finally, our measures of smoking, drinking, and drug use indicate whether the woman ever engaged in these practices during the focal pregnancy. The drug-use variable is a dichotomy based on two separate questions about the use of marijuana and the use of cocaine: a 0 indicates that neither marijuana nor cocaine was used during the focal pregnancy, and a 1 indicates use of one or both of the drugs. Because of the sensitive nature of the information, the questions on stressful life events and unhealthy behaviors were answered privately using a self-administered questionnaire.

In addition, we analyze two dichotomous measures of infant health, low birth weight and infant mortality. Low birth weight is an important risk factor for infant mortality and a variety of childhood illnesses and health problems. Using the birth weight recorded on the birth certificate, infants are classified as low birth weight if they weighed less than 2,500 grams at birth and normal birth weight if they weighed at least 2,500 grams at birth. Infant mortality is defined as death during the first year of an infant's life.

Predictor Variables

Scholars concerned with the assimilation process typically focus on generation or duration of residence (for the foreign-born). We combine these approaches by distinguishing women who were born in the US from women who were born in Puerto Rico—and, among the latter group, differentiating those who migrated to the US during early childhood from those who migrated at a later age. Although our data set allows us to determine whether mainland-born women are second- or third-generation US residents (i.e., whether their parents were born in the US), the vast majority of the US-born women in our sample (94% of those with valid data on parents' birthplaces) belong to the second generation. Thus, the distinction between mainland- and island-born women essentially captures generational status. Early migrants are those who were born in Puerto Rico and moved to the US on or before their tenth birthday, whereas late migrants are island-born women who moved to the US after their tenth birthday. In general, one would expect late migrants to be the least assimilated and US-born women to be the most assimilated of the three migration status groups.

Demographic and family background characteristics of each woman include her age, number of children, whether she lived with both parents at the age of 14, and whether her family received public assistance before she reached the age of 14.[13] Both age and the number of children are measured as of the beginning of the focal pregnancy.

Three measures of human capital and financial resources are included: educational attainment, employment experience, and household income. Education measures the highest grade of school completed by the woman. Employment experience is a dichotomous indicator of whether the woman had ever been employed outside the home prior to the focal pregnancy. To measure household income, women were asked to indicate which of 13 categories best represented their total household income around the time the focal baby was conceived. These categories were recoded to their midpoints, and income is treated as an interval variable.

Three variables measure the availability of social support during the pregnancy. Union status indicates whether the woman coresided with a partner and the legal status of the union. It is measured as of the beginning of the pregnancy and is coded into three categories: not living with a partner, living with a partner informally, and living with a partner to whom she is legally married. In addition, each woman provided information on all other individuals living with her at the beginning of the pregnancy. From this household roster, we created a measure of whether extended family members lived in the household. Last, the women were asked how long it would have taken various relatives to travel from their homes to the woman's home during the period in which she was pregnant. The relatives included in this question sequence were the respondent's mother, father, and brothers and sisters, as well as her partner's mother, father, and brothers and sisters. To measure the density of social support from relatives potentially available nearby, we constructed a measure of the number of these relatives reported to be living within one-half hour's distance of the respondent.

A Latino cultural orientation also has been identified as potentially protective of pregnant women (Cobas et al. 1996; Scribner and Dwyer 1989). To measure the extent to which respondents were embedded in the Latino community, we include three variables. The first is an additive index constructed from three questions regarding the respondent's use of English versus Spanish at home, with friends, and when watching television. The responses to each question (English most of the time; Spanish and English about equally; Spanish most of the time) were coded from 1 to 3, with 3 indicating Spanish dominance. The resulting index, which ranges from 3 to 9, is reliable, with a Cronbach's alpha of .77. We also include separate measures of the ethnic composition of the respondents' friends and neighborhoods. Responses range from 1 to 5, with 1 indicating "all non-Latinos" and 5 indicating "all Latinos."

In addition to individual attributes, neighborhood characteristics play an important role in theories about the factors underlying diverse pathways of assimilation. To examine the effect of the neighborhood environment on the stressful life events and health behaviors of pregnant Puerto Rican women, we coded the residential addresses provided on the birth certificates to the census tract level. We constructed indicators of the socioeconomic environment of each census tract from data available at the tract level in the Summary Tape Files of the 1990 census (US Bureau of the Census 1992). Included among those indicators are percentage of the population 16 years old and over in the labor force, percentage of the civilian labor force 16 years old and over unemployed, percentage of adults 25 years old and over with less than a high school education, median household income, percentage of households (with children under 18 years old) female-headed, and percentage of housing units owner-occupied. We also constructed measures of the ethnic and linguistic environment of the neighborhood: percentage of the population non-Latino black, percentage of the population Latino, percentage of the population 18–64 years old that does not speak English well or at all, and the percentage of households that are linguistically isolated.

Many of the above-mentioned neighborhood characteristics are highly intercorrelated. Indeed, their intercorrelations preclude inclusion of more than a few of the measures in the multivariate models. In lieu of arbitrarily selecting one measure over another, a principal-components factor analysis was performed (with varimax rotation) in order to determine the underlying structure of the 11 context measures. The factor analysis indicated that the context variables reflect two underlying dimensions. The first factor represents what might be called the *economic marginality* of the area. High factor loadings are generated by the labor-force participation rate, the percent unemployed, the median household income, the percent female-headed households, and the percent non-Latino black. The percent of adults with less than a high school education and the percent of housing units owner occupied also load moderately on this factor. The second factor depicts the *ethnic context*, with high factor loadings for the percent Latino, the percent that do not speak English well or at all, and the percentage of households that are linguistically isolated. The second factor also has a moderate loading for the percentage of adults with less than a high school education.[14]

RESULTS

Bivariate Analysis

Table 1 shows the bivariate relationships between generational status and each of the measures of women's lifestyles during pregnancy. Also shown is the percentage of low-birth-weight children for each generational status group.[15]

There are significant relationships between generation and five of the seven stressful life events. Of the mainland-born women, 22% reported that someone very close to them had a serious drinking or drug problem, compared to 10% of early migrants and 8% of late migrants. Similarly, mainland-born women are more likely to have had their husband or partner go to jail (8% versus 6% for early migrants and 3% for late migrants), to have been homeless (6% versus 3% for early migrants and 2% for late migrants), to have been in a physical fight (10% versus 5% for early migrants and 3% for late migrants), and to have been hit by their husband or partner (7% versus 2% for early migrants and 1% for late migrants). The higher level of overall exposure to stressful life events among the mainland-born is apparent in the significant relationship between generation and the total number of stressful events. In addition, subjective stress ratings are highest for US-born women.

Generational status is also related to smoking behavior during pregnancy. About 18% of mainland-born women and 17% of early migrants reported smoking while they were pregnant with the focal child. The rate of smoking for late migrants is considerably lower, at 7%. In contrast, generation is not significantly related to either drinking or drug use. The incidence of drug

TABLE 1
Stressful Life Events and Health Habits by Generational Status

	Generational Status			
	Puerto Rican-Born, Late Migrant	Puerto Rican-Born, Early Migrant	US-Born	Chi-Square/ F-test
Friend with drug problem	8.3	10.2	22.5	33.99***
Partner in jail	2.6	5.6	7.9	8.98*
Homeless	2.3	2.9	5.9	6.97*
Lost job	3.4	3.2	5.8	3.73
Too many bills	18.9	16.5	21.4	2.59
In physical fight	2.6	4.8	10.2	17.71***
Hit by partner	1.3	1.6	7.3	19.31***
Number of stressful events	.4	.4	.8	10.98***
Subjective stress	1.8	2.1	2.2	3.88*
Smoked	7.4	16.6	17.7	14.96***
Drank alcohol	2.5	6.9	4.3	4.85†
Used drugs	1.5	1.7	1.7	.05
Low birth weight	8.8	12.2	9.7	1.54

Note: F-test from one-way analysis of variance is presented for total number of stressful events and subjective stress.
†$p < .10$ *$p < .05$ **$p < .01$ ***$p < .001$

use is very low (less than 2%) for each of the three migration status groups. Consequently, drug use is dropped from consideration in the multivariate analyses that follow.

Also shown in Table 1 is the percentage of each group giving birth to a low-birth-weight infant. Although the overall relationship between generational status and low birth weight is not significant, the pattern for birth weight is consistent with the lifestyle results in that late migrants have the most favorable outcomes. However, it is early migrants rather than the US-born who exhibit the highest percentage of low-birth-weight infants.

Generational differences in the predictors included in the multivariate models are shown in Table 2. There are significant differences by generational status in all predictors except education and household income. Focusing first on family background, late migrants are less likely to have experienced family disruption during childhood than either early migrants or mainland-born women. About 68% of late migrants lived with both parents at the age of 14, compared to 53% of early migrants and 58% of mainland-born women. Despite these differences, a high percentage of each group received public assistance during childhood. About 60% of late migrants, 76% of early migrants,

TABLE 2
Means and Percentages for Independent Variables by Generational Status

	Generational Status			
	Puerto Rican-Born, Late Migrant	Puerto Rican-Born, Early Migrant	US-Born	Chi-Square/ F-test
Age	26.7	24.4	23.8	22.61***
Number of children	1.4	1.1	1.1	9.25***
Lived with both parents at 14	68.3	52.7	58.3	12.30**
Public assistance by 14	60.0	75.8	61.7	15.46***
Education	11.6	11.4	11.7	2.35†
Ever employed	55.5	62.2	70.3	18.99***
Household income	19,033	21,368	21,725	1.23
Union status				
Single	19.3	28.2	38.0	
Cohabiting	43.6	37.5	37.5	35.40***
Married	37.1	34.2	24.5	
Extended family	23.3	35.1	39.6	21.31***
Number of relatives nearby	4.1	4.1	4.2	6.71**
Language-use index	7.1	5.1	4.5	204.73***
Latino friends	3.8	3.5	3.4	24.95***
Latino neighbors	3.0	3.0	2.9	5.42**

Note: F-test from one-way analysis of variance is presented for age, number of children, education, household income, number of relatives nearby, language-use index, Latino friends, and Latino neighbors.
†$p < .10$ *$p < .05$ **$p < .01$ ***$p < .001$

and 62% of mainland-born women received public assistance during their childhood years.

There are few differences between the groups with respect to human and financial capital. Among our indicators, only employment experience prior to pregnancy differs significantly by migration status. Despite their higher mean age, late migrants are less likely to have worked before pregnancy (56%) than early migrants (62%) and mainland-born women (70%). This pattern may be related to group differences in union status. Only 19% of late migrants lived outside a coresidential union at the time they became pregnant, compared to 28% of early migrants and 38% of US-born women. Consistent with their high rate of singlehood, mainland-born women were the most likely to be living with extended kin. About 40% of the mainland-born lived in a household that included relatives other than a spouse/partner or children, compared to 23% of late migrants and 35% of early migrants. Finally, as one would expect, Spanish dominance and Latino friendships are more likely among late migrants than early migrants or US-born women.

MULTIVARIATE ANALYSIS: STRESSFUL LIFE EVENTS

Table 3 presents results from logistic regression models of stressful life events and negative health habits and ordinary least-squares regression models of the number of stressful life events and the respondent's subjective assessment of her stress level. Two models are shown for each dependent variable. Model 1 displays the bivariate relationship between generational status and the outcome variable. Model 2 adds individual and contextual predictors, thereby allowing assessment of the roles of family background, demographic characteristics, socioeconomic resources, social support, cultural orientation, and the neighborhood setting in the generational pattern found in model 1. For ease of interpretation, model coefficients have been transformed to odds ratios for the logistic regression models.[16]

Model 1 in Table 3 reexpresses the generational differences reviewed earlier (in the discussion of Table 1) in terms of odds ratios, using late migrants as the reference group. The higher risk of stressful life events faced by US-born women is readily apparent: Relative to late migrants, mainland-born women have significantly higher odds of having a friend or relative with a drinking/drug problem, having their husband/partner go to jail, being homeless, being in a physical fight, and being hit by their husband/partner. The odds of experiencing each of the first three events are about three times as high for mainland-born women as for late migrants. The odds ratios are even larger for being in a physical fight or being hit by the spouse/partner. For the former, the odds are four times as great, and for the latter the odds are six times as great for US-born women as for the reference group. The same pattern is evident for the summary measure of the total number of stressful life events experienced during the pregnancy.

Generational differences in subjective stress ratings, smoking, and alcohol use differ somewhat from the pattern shown for stressful life events. For the stressful life events, women who migrated to the US mainland during early childhood do not differ from those who migrated during adolescence or adulthood. However, early migrants rate their stress levels during pregnancy as higher than those of late migrants. Moreover, the odds of smoking are twice as high for early migrants as they are for late migrants, and the smoking behavior of early migrants resembles that of US-born women. The significant parameter estimate for alcohol use also suggests an increased risk for early migrants.

The most striking conclusion to be drawn from comparisons of model 1 and model 2 for each dependent variable is that controls for individual and neighborhood attributes have very little effect on the magnitude and statistical significance of the coefficients for generational status. Exceptions lie in the models for husband/partner in jail and alcohol use, in which controls for the full set of predictors reduce the coefficients for generation status to non-

TABLE 3
Models of Stressful Life Events and Health Habits

	Friend with Drug Problem		Partner in Jail		Homeless	
	(1)	(2)	(1)	(2)	(1)	(2)
Generation						
Late migrant						
Early migrant	1.26	1.16	2.25	1.45	1.29	1.45
US-born	3.22***	3.10***	3.29**	1.91	2.70*	3.14*
Age		.99		.96		.97
Number of children		.97		1.32*		1.46**
Lived with both parents at 14		.68*		1.10		.60
Public assistance by 14		1.00		1.36		1.01
Education		.92†		.78***		.96
Ever employed		1.31		1.27		1.45
Household income		.99*		1.00		.94**
Union status						
Single						
Cohabiting		1.54*		.88		.48*
Married		1.35		.34*		1.19
Extended family		.73		1.58		1.05
Number of relatives nearby		.98		.96		.86**
Language-use index		.99		.81*		1.02
Latino friends		.86		.74†		.94
Latino neighbors		.89		1.28†		1.28
Neighborhood economically marginal		1.11		1.49**		1.25
Neighborhood Latino		1.05		.76†		.70*
−2 Log-likelihood/R^2	1008.32	968.22	523.51	436.56	417.22	348.12
df	1130	1112	1125	1107	1128	1110
N	1,132	1,132	1,127	1,127	1,130	1,130

continued on next page

significance. Overall, however, compositional differences with respect to the variables included in model 2 cannot account for the higher risk of stressful life events and poor health behaviors of mainland-born women compared to that of late migrants. Thus, despite the fact that our models include a wide array of risk factors (e.g., limited financial and human capital, residence in disadvantaged neighborhoods) and protective factors (e.g., social support and a Latino cultural orientation) hypothesized to influence generational decline, we are unable to account for the strikingly higher risk of most stressful life

TABLE 3 *(continued)*
Models of Stressful Life Events and Health Habits

	Lost Job		Too Many Bills		In Physical Fight	
	(1)	(2)	(1)	(2)	(1)	(2)
Generation						
Late migrant						
Early migrant	.93	.96	.85	.89	1.92	1.80
US-born	1.76	1.56	1.17	1.29	4.32***	4.50**
Age		.99		1.00		.91**
Number of children		1.21		1.15*		1.31*
Lived with both						
parents at 14		.37**		1.03		.82
Public assistance						
by 14		.80		1.76**		1.92*
Education		1.13		1.01		.96
Ever employed		10.47***		2.44***		1.08
Household income		.97**		.99		1.02†
Union status						
Single						
Cohabiting		.64		.76		.80
Married		.92		.69		.36*
Extended family		.39*		.52**		.98
Number of relatives						
nearby		.99		1.01		.91*
Language-use index		1.13		1.03		1.06
Latino friends		.79		1.08		.87
Latino neighbors		.90		1.01		1.32*
Neighborhood						
economically						
marginal		1.04		1.07		1.45**
Neighborhood Latino		1.26		.96		.80†
−2 Log-likelihood/R²	436.81	362.69	1136.98	1074.02	593.38	523.32
df	1127	1109	1132	1114	1129	1111
N	1,129	1,129	1,134	1,134	1,131	1,131

events experienced by US-born Puerto Rican women compared to that experienced by women born in Puerto Rico.

Nonetheless, it is important to investigate whether these risk and protective factors are themselves related to the outcome variables. To do so, we use model 2 to identify the predictors that exhibit the most consistent relationships with the dependent variables. Among the background variables, the number of children a woman has is the most consistent predictor of the outcomes. The number of children is positively related to four specific stressful life events, the stressful life events index, perceived stress, and smoking. But

TABLE 3 *(continued)*
Models of Stressful Life Events and Health Habits

	Hit by Partner		Number of Stressful Events		Subjective Stress	
	(1)	(2)	(1)	(2)	(1)	(2)
Generation						
Late migrant	—	—	—	—	—	—
Early migrant	1.24	1.19	.05	−.00	.32*	.28†
US-born	5.95**	7.08**	.41***	.36***	.48***	.39**
Age		1.00		−.01		.00
Number of children		1.12		.09***		.09*
Lived with both parents at 14		1.01		−.14*		.01
Public assistance by 14		1.98†		.16*		−.11
Education		.90		−.01		−.04
Ever employed		1.43		.26***		.38***
Household income		1.00		−.004*		−.00
Union status						
Single		—		—		—
Cohabiting		1.47		−.07		.11
Married		.16*		−.15†		−.14
Extended family		.81		−.16*		−.18†
Number of relatives nearby		.95		−.02†		−.02
Language-use index		1.02		.00		−.06†
Latino friends		1.06		−.03		.09†
Latino neighbors		1.21		.01		.02
Neighborhood economically marginal		.86		.09**		.07
Neighborhood Latino		.94		−.05†		.02
−2 Log-likelihood/R^2	427.88	378.66	.036	.117	.018	.061
df	1130	1112	1119	1101	1144	1126
N	1,132	1,132	1,121	1,121	1,146	1,146

continued on next page

while the number of children signals risk, it is unlikely to be related to some negative outcomes in a causal manner. Human capital and financial resources are more important in terms of arguments about the causes of generational decline. Among the measures of human and financial capital, household income shows the most regular relationships with the stressful life events. Income is negatively related to having a friend or relative with a drug or alcohol problem, homelessness, job loss, and the total number of stressful life events.

TABLE 3 *(continued)*
Models of Stressful Life Events and Health Habits

	Smoked		Drank Alcohol	
	(1)	(2)	(1)	(2)
Generation				
Late migrant				
Early migrant	2.41*	2.61**	2.87*	2.21
US-born	2.88***	2.52**	1.75	1.21
Age		1.03		.96
Number of children		1.31***		1.15
Lived with both parents at 14		.85		.72
Public assistance by 14		.90		.82
Education		.87**		.88
Ever employed		1.02		.90
Household income		1.02		1.02†
Union status				
Single				
Cohabiting		.95		1.33
Married		.32***		.72
Extended family		.54**		.42*
Number of relatives nearby		.96		.99
Language-use index		.88*		.87
Latino friends		.79*		.81
Latino neighbors		1.08		.96
Neighborhood economically marginal		1.37**		1.24
Neighborhood Latino		1.24*		1.15
–2 Log-likelihood/R^2	853.96	792.98	385.73	360.56
df	1085	1067	1079	1061
N	1,087	1,087	1,081	1,081

Notes: Logistic regression was used to estimate all models except those for number of stressful events and subjective stress rating. Models for the latter two variables were estimated with ordinary least-squares regression. The coefficients from the logistic regression models are expressed as odds ratios.
†$p < .10$ *$p < .05$ **$p < .01$ ***$p < .001$

These relationships lend support to the argument that poverty contributes to many detrimental circumstances and behaviors.

At the same time, living with extended family members appears to be an important protective factor. Women who lived with extended family members at the beginning of pregnancy are less likely to have lost their job, had too many bills, experienced many stressful life events, smoked, or drank during pregnancy. Using the .10 level of significance, living with extended family members is also negatively related to subjective stress levels. Living with extended family members appears to be more important to the outcomes we examine than the individual-level measures of Latino cultural orientation or the neighborhood measure of Latino ethnic context. In addition, living in an economically marginal neighborhood is positively related to having a husband/partner go to jail, being in a physical fight, the total number of stressful life events, and smoking, net of the full set of predictors in model 2.

MULTIVARIATE ANALYSIS: LOW BIRTH WEIGHT AND INFANT MORTALITY

To this point, we have demonstrated that the risk of stressful life events and negative health habits during pregnancy is higher for mainland-born women than for women who migrated to the mainland after age 10. Women who migrated during early childhood are similar to late migrants on most outcomes, although they have higher subjective stress ratings and an elevated risk of smoking and drinking during pregnancy. Both the extent to which similar generational patterns are found for birth outcomes and the role of stressful life events and health habits in producing the generational patterns are examined in Table 4. The first three columns of the table present models of infant birth weight (low versus normal), and the last four columns present models of infant mortality.[17]

The first column in Table 4 shows the bivariate relationship between generational status and low birth weight. The odds of bearing a low-birth-weight infant are almost twice as high for early migrants as for late migrants. Moreover, the coefficient for US-born women is almost significant ($p = .097$) and is in the expected direction. This generational pattern is consistent with the results for stressful life events and health habits in that late migrants have the most favorable outcomes. However, the significant coefficient for early migrants suggests that the risk of low birth weight increases more rapidly with time in the US than the risk of experiencing stressful life events.

Model 2 adds controls for the full set of covariates included in the multivariate models of stressful life events.[18] Net of these controls, the pattern for generational status remains largely unchanged. In model 3, stressful life events, subjective stress levels, and health habits are controlled. Although women's subjective stress ratings are strongly related to the birth weight of their offspring, inclusion of the measures of stress and health habits does not attenuate the parameter estimate for early migrants.[19] Thus, the generational differences in stress and health habits observed in Tables 1 and 3 do not appear to play a major role in accounting for generational differences in low birth weight.

Models 1–3 for infant mortality parallel models 1–3 for low birth weight. Model 4 adds low birth weight as a predictor of infant mortality to determine its role as a mediating factor. Both before (model 1) and after (model 2) the introduction of controls for social and economic characteristics of women and their neighborhoods, both early migrants and US-born women have odds of

TABLE 4
Logistic Regression Models of Low Birth Weight and Infant Mortality

	Low Birth Weight		
	(1)	(2)	(3)
Generation			
Late migrant			
Early migrant	1.76**	1.79*	1.79*
US-born	1.33†	1.34	1.27
Age			
<20		1.27	1.25
20–34			
35+		.89	.90
Infant birth order			
1		.99	1.07
2–3			
4+		1.14	1.00
Lived with both parents at 14		.98	1.03
Public assistance by 14		.83	.83
Education		.98	.99
Ever employed		.68**	.63**
Household income		1.00	1.00
Union status			
Single			
Cohabiting		1.05	1.06
Married		1.09	1.15
Extended family		1.06	1.08
Number of relatives			
nearby		.95*	.96*
Language-use index		.98	.99
Latino friends		.93	.93
Latino neighbors		1.11†	1.11†
Neighborhood economically			
marginal		1.03	1.00
Neighborhood Latino		1.04	1.04
Number of stressful events			1.11
Subjective stress			1.18***
Smoked			1.25
Drank alcohol			.75
–2 Log-likelihood	1417.32	1380.42	1357.89
df	1041	1021	1017
N	1,044	1,044	1,044

TABLE 4 *(continued)*
Logistic Regression Models of Low Birth Weight and Infant Mortality

	Infant Mortality			
	(1)	(2)	(3)	(4)
Generation				
Late migrant				
Early migrant	2.19**	1.95*	1.84*	1.30
US-born	1.74**	1.81*	1.56†	1.31
Age				
<20		1.20	1.24	1.00
20–34				
35+		.95	.94	.97
Infant birth order				
1		1.10	1.22	1.17
2–3				
4+		1.40	1.20	1.11
Lived with both parents at 14		.66**	.72*	.73*
Public assistance by 14		.80	.80	.87
Education		.94	.95	.96
Ever employed		.69*	.66*	.82
Household income		.99	.99	.99
Union status				
Single		-	-	-
Cohabiting		1.20	1.21	1.30
Married		1.15	1.31	1.35
Extended family		1.02	1.04	1.07
Number of relatives nearby		1.01	1.02	1.02
Language-use index		.99	1.02	1.02
Latino friends		.95	.96	1.04
Latino neighbors		1.25**	1.24**	1.13
Neighborhood economically marginal		.88†	.84*	.86*
Neighborhood Latino		.97	.96	.95
Number of stressful events			1.05	1.00
Subjective stress			1.43***	1.20**
Smoked			1.61	1.41†
Drank alcohol			1.18	1.37
Infant low birth weight				14.65***
–2 Log-likelihood	1740.24	1556.82	1503.11	1196.71
df	1324	1304	1300	1299
N	1,327	1,327	1,327	1,327

Note: The coefficients from the logistic regression models are expressed as odds ratios.
†$p < .10$ *$p < .05$ **$p < .01$ ***$p < .001$

infant mortality that are roughly twice as high as the odds for late migrants. This pattern diverges from that for birth weight in that US-born women differ significantly from late migrants.

Model 3 adds measures of lifestyle and health habits during pregnancy to the model of infant death. High self-reported stress levels and smoking are positively related to infant mortality. The coefficients for generational status, however, change very little when stress and health habits are controlled. Although the odds ratio for US-born women is reduced to 1.6 and is no longer significant in model 3 ($p = .083$), it is clear that these factors play a very limited role in explaining why the offspring of childhood migrants and US-born women have a relatively high risk of dying during infancy. As has been documented amply in prior studies, low birth weight is a major risk factor for infant mortality: Model 4 shows that the odds of death for low-birth-weight infants are roughly 15 times as high as those for normal-birth-weight infants. In addition, when low birth weight is added to the model, there are no remaining differences between the generation groups in the risk of infant mortality.

SUMMARY AND CONCLUSIONS

During the last several years, there has been a great deal of interest in understanding why infant health outcomes deteriorate across generations in some immigrant groups. Although this paradoxical pattern has been confirmed by numerous studies, less is known about the mechanisms through which assimilation compromises infant health. Investigations have been limited by the lack of information in many national data sets (e.g., the vital-records-based data files produced by the National Center for Health Statistics) on multiple components of women's lifestyles during pregnancy and on key explanatory factors. Moreover, because the literature has emphasized the Mexican-origin population, little is known about the influence of assimilation on the prenatal behavior of women in other ethnic groups.

This study focuses on the effects of the migration and assimilation processes on the lifestyles, health habits, and birth outcomes of Puerto Rican women. In particular, we assess how pregnant women's exposure to stressful life events and their substance-use patterns vary by nativity and age at the time of migration. The implications of stress and health habits for low birth weight and infant mortality—and the role of these factors in explaining generational differences in the risk of low birth weight and infant death—also are addressed. We examine these issues within the context of broader theories about the nature of the assimilation process and the circumstances under which a pattern of deteriorating outcomes across generations occurs.

Our analysis shows striking generational differences in stressful life events and health habits during pregnancy, with mainland-born women more likely to experience adverse events and to have harmful health habits than island-born women. The stressful life events exhibiting this pattern range from having a close friend/relative with a serious drug or alcohol problem to being physically abused by a spouse/partner. The major health habit for which the pattern holds is cigarette smoking, although early migrants (those who migrated before age 10) have rates of smoking during pregnancy that resemble those of US-born women. Multivariate models of the stressful life events and health habits include a wide range of predictors identified in theories of generational decline (e.g., human capital, financial resources, social support, Latino cultural orientation, neighborhood characteristics). But despite the rich array of independent variables, we are unable to explain the generational pattern.

Our analysis of infant health shows that high levels of stress elevate the risk of low birth weight and infant mortality. However, neither birth weight nor infant mortality varies by generational status in a manner identical to stressful life events or subjective evaluations of stress. On the one hand, the most recent migrants from Puerto Rico experience the fewest stressful life events, report the lowest levels of distress, and are the least likely to smoke or drink alcohol during pregnancy. US-born Puerto Rican women are the most likely to experience stressful life events, to rate their stress levels as high, and to smoke during pregnancy—and their infants have a higher risk of infant mortality than those of recent migrants. On the other hand, women who migrated to the US during early childhood have a favorable profile with respect to stress, but their offspring have rates of low birth weight and infant mortality that are markedly higher than those of women who migrated later in life. Thus, birth outcomes (and smoking) appear to worsen within the first generation, while exposure to stressful life events does not. Although the pattern for birth outcomes suggests that negative assimilation is occurring within the first generation,[20] we are unable to explain the generational pattern in terms of the risk and protective factors considered in our models.

An alternative explanation of the favorable infant health outcomes of late migrants focuses on migration selectivity: Women who migrate during adolescence or early adulthood may be positively selected on traits that are related to the health and survival of their offspring. For example, migration may be undertaken by women who have especially good physical or mental health, strong motivation to succeed, or unusual resourcefulness. Such positive selectivity may not characterize early migrants because childhood moves generally result from the volition of family members other than the woman herself (e.g., parents). Although investigation of this issue is beyond the scope of the present study, the selectivity hypothesis provides another possible interpretation of the generational patterns we have documented. Investigation of the role of selectivity is therefore an important next step in our research on the infant health outcomes of mainland Puerto Ricans.

Overall, the patterns we have documented are consistent with those of a growing number of studies that find that traditional indicators of assimilation (i.e., duration of residence and generation) are not always positively related to health and well-being (Institute of Medicine/National Research Council 1998). Understanding the circumstances giving rise to this apparent generational decline should continue to be a high priority for research. Investigations of maternal and infant health among immigrant groups have largely focused on behaviors with direct effects on health outcomes, such as smoking. We have demonstrated that such health-risk behaviors exhibit patterns that are similar to those for a much wider array of lifestyle factors. Future research on the epidemiological paradox would benefit from greater attention to the broader set of social conditions that define the prospects and daily realities confronted by first- and second-generation women.

NOTES

1. This broad-brush description necessarily oversimplifies some of the complexities of assimilation theory. For example, Gordon (1964) distinguishes between the Anglo conformity and melting pot models of assimilation. The Anglo conformity model assumes that immigrants take up the culture and characteristics of the Anglo-Saxon majority, while the melting pot model proposes that American society represents a blending of the traditions and traits of many ethnic groups. In addition, some early literature points to the persistence of ethnic subcultures as well as to variation in the nature and pace of assimilation across ethnic groups (Shibutani and Kwan 1965).

2. Immigration from Southeast Asian countries, such as Vietnam and Cambodia, is too recent for comparisons to be made between the reproductive outcomes of foreign-born and native-born women. However, one recent study provides evidence that the generational pattern is not restricted to the Mexican-origin population. Based on national data, Landale, Oropesa, and Gorman (1999) show that in nine of 10 ethnic groups examined (Chinese, Filipinos, other Asians, Mexicans, Puerto Ricans, Cubans, Central/South Americans, non-Latino blacks, and non-Latino whites), infants of foreign-born mothers had lower rates of low birth weight and infant mortality than infants of native-born mothers. In most groups the magnitude of the nativity differential is considerably smaller than that found for Mexicans.

3. Puerto Ricans, Native Americans, and African Americans were identified in *Healthy People 2000* (US Department of Health and Human Services 1991) as groups in need of special attention because of their poor infant health outcomes.

Although technically considered internal migrants due to the commonwealth status of Puerto Rico, Puerto Rican migrants to the US are more similar to immigrants than to internal migrants in that they are Spanish speaking, frequently lack proficiency in English, and are culturally distinct from the US mainstream. Therefore, their adaptation to the US mainland is generally analyzed within an assimilation framework.

4. First generation refers to foreign-born persons who immigrated to the US during childhood or adulthood. Second generation refers to the US-born offspring of foreign-born parents.

5. See Massey (1993), Moore (1989), and Tienda (1989) for discussions of the applicability of the term underclass to the mainland Puerto Rican population.

6. The Linked Birth-Infant Death Data Sets contain information from the birth certificate for all births occurring in the US in a given year and information from the death certificate for all infants born in that year who died before their first birthday. They are compiled by the National Center for Health Statistics.

7. The study was funded by the National Institute of Child Health and Human Development, the Maternal and Child Health Bureau, and the Centers for Disease Control. The data were collected by the Institute for Survey Research at Temple University under a subcontract from the Population Research Institute, Pennsylvania State University.

8. The included US states are those with the greatest number of births to Puerto Rican women each year. In 1994 and 1995, 72.3% of all births to mainland Puerto Rican women occurred in these states. The state of New York is divided into two separate vital statistics reporting areas, New York City and the remainder of the state. Permission to conduct the study was received from New York City but could not be obtained from the state of New York. New York cases are therefore restricted to births and deaths occurring in New York City.

9. Infants weighing less than 2,500 grams were oversampled to allow for analyses of the determinants of low birth weight. The final weights are based on the probability of selection, nonresponse, and a poststratification adjustment. They therefore adjust for the higher probability of selection given to low-birth-weight infants.

10. An exception to this practice lies in predictors with 5% or more of the cases missing a valid value. Cases defined as missing on such variables were assigned the mean, and a dummy variable indicating missing status was included in the regression analysis.

11. The number of cases varies somewhat across various parts of our analysis because the amounts of missing data differ on the dependent variables we analyze.

12. Physical abuse by the partner might be regarded as a specific instance of the previous item, involvement in a physical fight. Although responses to these items indicate some overlap, they also suggest that they are largely distinct. Only one-half of the women who were abused by their husband/partner answered that they were in a physical fight during pregnancy. Of those who were in a fight, less than one-third indicated abuse by the husband/partner.

13. At an earlier stage of the analysis, several additional measures of family background (e.g., mother's and father's education) were considered. However, none of these additional variables significantly improved the fit of the models, and they were therefore dropped.

14. Results from the factor analysis are available from the authors upon request.

15. The results in Tables 1, 2, and 3 are based on weighted data, with the weights adjusted to retain the original sample size. Infant mortality rates cannot be derived from the birth sample because there are too few death cases to produce stable estimates. Although the oversample of infant deaths is useful for multivariate analyses of infant mortality, it is not appropriate for the construction of infant mortality rates.

16. Although we estimated models adding various sets of variables sequentially, they are not presented here because of space limitations. The results for generational status and other individual-level predictors are very similar in models restricted to individual-level variables and the full model in Table 3.

17. The study design for the PRMIHS entailed sampling within categories of the two dependent variables, infant birth weight (low versus normal) and infant mortality. Consequently, each of these outcome variables in the study is fixed by stratification. Following Fears and Brown (1986), our analyses of low birth weight and infant mortality adjust for this sampling procedure through inclusion of a fixed "offset" term in the logistic regression equations. The "offset" term is based on the sampling fractions for each stratum as well as the total number of respondents in the stratum.

18. The mother's age is included in categorical form because prior research has demonstrated that age has a nonlinear relationship with low birth weight. Both younger mothers and older mothers have an elevated risk of having a low-birth-weight infant. In addition, we include infant birth order in categorical form in lieu of the number of children. In general, first births and higher-order births (e.g., 4+) have a higher risk of low birth weight than others.

19. When the subjective stress rating is excluded from the model, the coefficient for the total number of stressful life events is significant and positive.

20. See Guendelman and English (1995) for similar results for Mexican-origin women.

REFERENCES

Alba, Richard, and Victor Nee. 1997. Rethinking assimilation for a new era of immigration. *International Migration Review* 31:826–74.

Aneshensel, Carol S. 1992. Social stress: Theory and research. *Annual Review of Sociology* 18:15–38.

Bean, Frank, and Marta Tienda. 1987. *The Hispanic Population of the United States.* Russell Sage Foundation.

Chomitz, Virginia R., Lilian W. Y. Cheung, and Ellice Lieberman. 1995. The role of lifestyle in preventing low birth weight. *Future of Children* 5:121–38.

Cobas, Jose A., Hector Balcazar, Mary B. Benin, Verna M. Keith, and Yinong Chong. 1996. Acculturation and low-birthweight infants among Latino women. *American Journal of Public Health* 86:394–96.

Collins, James W., and David K. Shay. 1994. Prevalence of low birth weight among Hispanic infants with United States-born and foreign-born mothers: The effect of urban poverty. *American Journal of Epidemiology* 139:184–92.

Fears, Thomas R., and Charles C. Brown. 1986. Logistic regression methods for retrospective case-control studies using complex sampling procedures. *Biometrics* 42:955–60.

Fennelly, Katherine. 1992. Sexual activity and childbearing among Hispanic adolescents in the United States. Pp. 335–52 in *Early Adolescence: Perspectives on Research, Policy and Intervention,* edited by R. Lerner et al. Erlbaum.

Gans, Herbert J. 1992. Second-generation decline: Scenarios for the economic and ethnic futures of the post–1965 American immigrants. *Ethnic and Racial Studies* 15:173–92.

Gordon, Milton M. 1964. *Assimilation in American Life.* Oxford University Press.

Guendelman, Sylvia, and Barbara Abrams. 1995. Dietary intake among Mexican-American women: Generational differences and a comparison with white non-Hispanic women. American Journal of Public Health 85:20–25.

Guendelman, Sylvia. 1995. Immigrants may hold clues to protecting health during pregnancy: Exploring a paradox: *Wellness Lecture Series,* Vol. 5. University of California.

Guendelman, Sylvia, and Paul B. English. 1995. Effect of United States residence on birth outcomes among Mexican immigrants: An exploratory study. *American Journal of Epidemiology* 142:S30–S38.

Harris, Kathleen M. 1999. The health status and risk behavior of adolescents in immigrant families. Pp. 286–347 in *Children of Immigrants: Health, Adjustment, and Public Assistance,* edited by Donald J. Hernandez. National Academy Press.

Institute of Medicine/National Research Council. 1998. *From Generation to Generation: The Health and Well-Being of Children in Immigrant Families.* National Academy Press.

Kaplan, Mark S., and Gary Marks. 1990. Adverse effects of acculturation: Psychological distress among Mexican American young adults. *Social Science Medicine* 31:1313–19.

Krieger, Nancy, Diane L. Rowley, Allen A. Herman, Byllye Avery, and Mona T. Phillips. 1993. Racism, sexism, and social class: Implications for studies of health, disease, and well-being. *American Journal of Preventive Medicine 9* (supp.):82–122.

Landale, Nancy S., R. S. Oropesa, and Bridget Gorman. 1999. Immigration and infant health: Birth outcomes of immigrant and native women. Pp. 244–85 in *Children of Immigrants: Health, Adjustment, and Public Assistance,* National Research Council and Institute of Medicine, edited by Donald J. Hernandez. National Academy Press.

Lemann, Nicholas. 1991. The other underclass. *Atlantic Monthly* 268(Dec.), pp. 96–110.

Massey, Douglas S. 1993. Latinos, poverty, and the underclass: A new agenda for research. *Hispanic Journal of Behavioral Sciences* 15:449–75.

McLean, Diane E., Kendra Hatfield-Timajchy, Phyllis A. Wingo, and R. Louise Floyd. 1993. Psychosocial Measurement: Implications for the study of preterm delivery in black women. *American Journal of Preventive Medicine* 9:39–81.

Moore, Joan. 1989. Is there a Hispanic underclass? *Social Science Quarterly* 70:265–84.

Oropesa, R.S., and Bridget K. Gorman.1998. Ethnicity, immigration and the tie that binds Paper presented at conference on Perspectives on Marriage and Cohabitation, National Institute of Child Health and Human Development, Bethesda, Maryland, June 29.

Oropesa, R. S., and Nancy S. Landale. 1997. Immigrant legacies: Ethnicity, generation, and children's familial and economic lives. *Social Science Quarterly* 78:399–416.

Park, Robert E. 1950. *Race and Culture*. Free Press.

Park, Robert E., and Ernest W. Burgess. 1921. *Introduction to the Science of Sociology*. University of Chicago Press.

Portes, Alejandro, and Min Zhou. 1993. The new second generation: Segmented assimilation and its variants. *Annals of the American Academy of Political and Social Sciences* 530:7496.

Rivera-Batiz, Francisco L., and Carlos E. Santiago. 1996. Island paradox: Puerto Rico in the 1990s. Russell Sage Foundation.

Rumbaut, Ruben G. 1997. Assimilation and its discontents: Between rhetoric and reality. *International Migration Review* 31:923–60.

Rumbaut, Ruben G., and John R. Weeks. 1989. Infant health among Indochinese refugees: patterns of infant mortality, birthweight, and prenatal care in comparative perspective. *Research in the Sociology of Health Care* 8:137–96.

Sandefur, Gary D., and Marta Tienda. 1988. Introduction: Social policy and the minority experience. Pp. 1–22 in *Divided Opportunities: Minorities, Poverty, and Social Policy*, edited by Gary D. Sandefur and Marta Tienda. Plenum Press.

Scribner, Richard, and James H. Dwyer. 1989. Acculturation and low birthweight among Latinos in the Hispanic HANES. *American Journal of Public Health* 79:1263–67.

Shibutani, Tamotsu, and Kian M. Kwan. 1965. *Ethnic Stratification*. Macmillan.

Tienda, Marta. 1989. Puerto Ricans and the underclass debate: Evidence for structural explanations of labor market performance. *Annals of the American Academy of Political and Social Science* 501:105–19.

Torres, Andres, and Clara E. Rodriguez. 1991. Latino research and policy: The Puerto Rican case. Pp. 247–64 in *Hispanics in the Labor Force: Issues and Policy*, edited by Edwin Meléndez, Clara E. Rodríguez, and Janis B. Figueroa. Plenum Press.

US Bureau of the Census. 1992. Census of population and housing, 1990: Summary tape file 3 on cd-rom technical documentation. Bureau of the Census.

US Department of Health and Human Services. 1991. *Healthy People 2000: National Health Promotion and Disease Prevention Objectives*. Public Health Service.

Williams, Ronald L., Nancy Binkin, and Elizabeth J. Clingman. 1986. Pregnancy outcomes among Spanish-surname women in California. *American Journal of Public Health* 76:38791.

Zambrana, Ruth E, Susan C. M. Scrimshaw, Nancy Collins, and Christine Dunkel-Schetter. 1997. Prenatal health behaviors and psychosocial risk factors in pregnant women of Mexican origin: The role of acculturation. *American Journal of Public Health* 87:1022–26.

Zhou, Min. 1997. Segmented assimilation: Issues, controversies, and recent research on the new second generation. *International Migration Review* 31:975–1008.

Nativity, Duration of Residence, Citizenship, and Access to Health Care for Hispanic Children

T. Elizabeth Durden

INTRODUCTION

This study considers the variation in access to regular sources of health care of children among major Hispanic subpopulations within the United States. Importantly, it takes into consideration the impact of the immigration status of the mother, namely nativity status, duration of residence within the US, and citizenship status, on children's access to health care.

Understanding access to health care is important in that it adds to our awareness of how well various Hispanic groups are being incorporated into the formal medical system of the US Differences between Hispanic groups may exist, originating in specific socioeconomic circumstances and geopolitical realities which produced the distinctive migration and incorporation experience of each Hispanic group within the United States (Novello et al. 1991; Durden 2007). These individual subgroup experiences may affect the medical care access and services utilized.

Overall, the literature on access to health care among Hispanic children ascertains that in comparison to non-Hispanic whites, Hispanics are less likely to receive care and are more likely to receive inferior care (Lieu et al. 1993, Weigers et al. 1998; Flores et al. 1999; Guendelman and Wagner 2000; Wei and Krauss 2000; Scott and Ni 2004). With a few exceptions of note (see LeClere et al. 1994, Weinick et al. 2000), the social demographic research on access to

T. Elizabeth Durden: "Nativity, Duration of Residence, Citizenship, and Access to Health Care for Hispanic Children," first published in *International Migration Review*, vol. 41, num. 2 (Summer 2007): 537–45.

health care for children is repeatedly limited by not including specific Hispanic ethnicity as well as immigration measures including nativity, duration, and citizenship. This research note will attempt to address these oversights.

DATA, MEASURES, AND METHODS

Data

Obtained from the Sample Child File Supplement of the National Health Interview Survey (NHIS), the data used in this research have been merged from the years 1999–2001 (Durden 2007). The NHIS maintains continuous cross-sectional sampling and interviewing throughout each year. The NHIS is an ideal resource for this study in that the annual response rate of the NHIS is greater than 90 percent of the eligible households in the sample, and, since 1995, both Black and Hispanic households have been oversampled. The sample for this study is restricted to children aged 0–17 who were identified as Hispanic, non-Hispanic white, or non-Hispanic black, which yields an unweighted sample size of 38,182. Excluded are all children of other race/ethnic categories.

Measures

Access to a regular source of usual health care is the outcome variable. In this study, access to care is measured by whether or not a respondent reported having a usual source of care. Measuring access to care as having a usual source of care is the standard measure used by health researchers (Weinick and Krauss 2000). A parent or guardian is asked, "Is there a place your child usually goes to when they are sick or need advice about their health?"

Independent variables include race/ethnicity, the immigration status of the mother, demographic variables, and socioeconomic factors. Race/ethnic categories include Mexican/Mexican American, Puerto Rican, Cuban American, and Other Hispanic. The other racial/ethnic categories of non-Hispanic white (reference) and non-Hispanic black are included for comparison purposes. The immigration status of the mother—that is, nativity, duration of time in the United States, and citizenship status—is included in the model. This immigration status measure consists of seven categories (i.e., Lopez-Gonzalez et al. 2005; Durden and Hummer 2006), with US-born mothers serving as the reference. Additionally, demographic and socioeconomic factors are controlled in an attempt to understand the overall differences in access to care across groups. The demographic controls include age, sex, family structure of the child, geographic region, and metro/non-metro residence. Socioeconomic variables include mother's education, family income, and insurance status.

Statistical analysis

Logistic regression is used to model the relationship between the dependent and independent variables. The models are built progressively in order to better understand how the demographic, immigration status, and socioeconomic variables affect the association between race/ethnicity and access to

TABLE 1
Odds Ratios for the Effects of Demographic and Social Factors on a Usual
Source of Health Care among Race/Ethnic Groups, US Children Aged 0–17,
1999–2001

	Model 1	Model 2	Model 3
Race/ethnicity [Non-Hispanic White]			
Mexican American	0.25***	0.36***	0.64***
Puerto Rican	0.49**	0.58*	0.92
Cuban American	1.01	1.62	1.43
Other Hispanic	0.39***	0.60***	0.78
Non-Hispanic black	0.78**	0.79*	1.10
Duration and Citizenship of Mother [US-born]			
Less than five years and citizen		0.23***	0.33*
Less than five years and non-citizen		0.17***	0.28***
Five to nine years and citizen		0.39*	0.46
Five to nine years and non-citizen		0.43***	0.76
Ten or more years and citizen		0.81	0.87
Ten or more years and non-citizen		0.55***	0.84
Sex [Male]			
Female	0.97	0.97	0.96
Age (continuous in years)	0.94***	0.93***	0.93***
Family Structure [Married Parents]			
Mother only	0.72**	0.68***	1.02
Cohabitating adults	0.46***	0.45***	0.75*
Stepfamily	0.92	0.88	1.00
Other adults in family	0.63***	0.64***	0.85
Country Region [Northeast]			
Midwest	0.34***	0.32***	0.29***
South	0.23***	0.22***	0.25***
West	0.24***	0.23***	0.22***

continued

health care (Mirowsky 1999). The first model in this analysis estimates basic
race/ethnic differences in access to health care, controlling only for essen-
tial demographic variables. More complex models are built in a progressive
fashion and include the immigration status variables (nativity, duration, and
citizenship), socioeconomic status (SES), and insurance status (Durden and
Hummer 2006). Progressive adjustment effectively establishes that the primary variables of interest are associated, while fostering an understanding of
how additional variables affect the baseline relationship under consideration
(Frisbie et al. 2001; Durden 2007). The statistical package Sudaan is used to
control for design effects in the NHIS.

ACCESS TO HEALTH CARE RESULTS

Logistic regression coefficients in the form of odds ratios are presented in
Table 1. Odds ratios below one denote lower odds of regular access to a regular

TABLE 1 *(continued)*
Odds Ratios for the Effects of Demographic and Social Factors on a Usual Source of Health Care among Race/Ethnic Groups, US Children Aged 0–17, 1999–2001

	Model 1	Model 2	Model 3
Resident Local [Large Urban Area]			
Small urban area	1.04	0.99	1.02
Non-urban area	0.92	0.88	1.09
Education of Mother [College and Beyond]			
Up to 8th grade			0.42***
Some high school			0.57***
High school certificate			0.60***
Some college			0.75*
Unknown			0.45***
Income [$35,000 or more]			
Less than $9,999			0.72*
$10,000–19,999			0.60***
$20,000–34,999			0.67***
Income not reported			0.69***
Insurance [Private]			
Misc. government			0.47***
Not insured			0.17***

Notes: ***$p < 0.001$, **$p < 0.01$, *$p < 0.05$, N = 38.132

–2LL (Intercept Only)	16,611	16,611	16,611
–2LL (Full Model)	15,091	14,830	13,727
X^2	1,591.5	1,780.4	2,883.3
Degrees of Freedom	16	22	33

source of care in comparison to the reference; values above one denote higher odds of reporting access to a usual source of care in relation to the reference.

Model 1 investigates the basic relationship between race/ethnicity and access to a usual source of health care, including controls for basic demographic variables. Mexican American (odds ratios = 0.25), Puerto Rican (odds ratios = 0.49), and Other Hispanic (odds ratios = 0.39) children all display significantly lower odds of having access to a usual source of health care in comparison to non-Hispanic white children. The access to a regular source of medical care among different Hispanic groups illustrated in this first model generally reinforce findings of previous literature, which specify that Hispanic groups have less access to care (Zuvekas and Weinick 1999; Scott and Ni 2004).

Model 2 introduces nativity, duration, and citizenship, allowing for a test of the impact of the mothers immigration status on reports of usual access to medical care for children within the United States. The results visibly illustrate that the combined nativity, duration, and citizenship measure of the mother quite significantly affects her child's access to regular care. Model 2 shows that, despite the amount of time spent in the United States, children of all non-citizen mothers are much less likely to report access to a usual source of care than children of US-born mothers (odds ratios of 0.17, 0.43, and 0.55, respectively). Furthermore, children of foreign-born naturalized mothers who are in the country less than five years (odds ratios = 0.23) or five to nine years (odds ratios = 0.39) are also less likely to report access to a usual source of care in comparison to the reference group. Only children of naturalized foreign-born respondents who have been in the United States for ten or more years report no difference in comparison to children of US-born mothers to having access to a usual source of medical care.

The dramatic altering of race/ethnic differentials after controlling for the immigration measures is noteworthy. Results show that nativity, duration, and citizenship do affect access to care. Specifically, the immigration status measure in the model increases the odds of reporting access to a usual source of health care for all Hispanic subgroups compared to non-Hispanic whites. Comparing Model 1 to Model 2, noteworthy gains are made in decreasing the likelihood that non-Hispanic white children will have greater access to care than Hispanic children. The odds of access to a usual source of medical care increase for all Hispanic subgroups compared to non-Hispanic whites with the immigration status measure in the model. The models show, however, that all disparities are not explained as Mexican Americans (odds ratios = 0.36), Puerto Ricans (odds ratios = 0.58). and Other Hispanics (odds ratios = 0.60) are still less likely to report regular access to care, as compared to non-Hispanic whites, even after taking into account demographic and immigration status factors.

Model 3 builds on Model 2 by including socioeconomic status indicators, including education of the mother, household income, and health insurance measures. These SES variables radically alter the access to care differentials for the immigration status indicators. Only children of mothers in the country less than five years, regardless of citizenship status, are less likely to report a usual source of health care (odds ratios of 0.33 and 0.28, respectively). With the inclusion of the SES measures, the remainder of the citizenship-duration categories are no different in reporting access to a regular source of medical care than the reference.

With the inclusion of SES indicators, it is interesting to note that the coefficients of the race/ethnic variables considerably improve as compared to the previous model. Puerto Rican, Cuban American, Other Hispanic, and non-Hispanic black children report no difference in accessing a regular source of medical care in comparison to non-Hispanic white children. However, somewhat surprisingly, controlling for insurance and other socioeconomic indicators does not completely eliminate the gap for Mexican Americans in comparison to Non-Hispanic whites. Mexican American children are still only 64% as likely to have access to care as non-Hispanic whites.

CONCLUSION

While considerable research on mortality and health differentials across racial/ethnic subpopulations exists, demographic research on access to regular medical care for children among different segments of the population is not as elaborate, especially at the population level (LeClere et al. 1994; Weinick and Krauss 2000). Established in the literature is the heightened risk of decreased access to medical care among racial and ethnic minorities, with Hispanics substantially more likely than other racial/ethnic groups to lack a usual source of health care (Zuvekas and Weinick 1999; Weinick et al. 2000). Less clear is the particular role played by various immigration measures—namely nativity, duration, and citizenship—on accessing a regular source of medical care for children of Hispanic subgroups. Clearly, the results of this study show that there are differences in access to health care among Hispanic subgroup children, differences strongly influenced by the immigration status of the mother, as well as various SES indicators.

The nativity, duration, and citizenship status of the mother clearly explained the initial disparities in access to regular health care among children in the Hispanic subgroups. This research strongly documented that children of immigrant mothers who have greater incorporation into the United States (in regards to duration and naturalization) are more likely to reflect the same access to care patterns as the children of the native-born. These findings are not wholly unexpected, as nativity, duration of residence, and citizenship of Hispanics will hinder or facilitate access to medical care, as recent research has shown (LeClere et al. 1994; Shetterly et al. 1996; Thamer et al. 1997; Jang et al. 1998). The variables of nativity, duration, and citizenship may measure an integration process whereby immigrants become more incorporated into the US sociopolitical economic system. As immigrants gain greater knowledge of the health system, specifically as well as through either private insurance or government assistance, they are able to better utilize the health care system (Frisbie et al. 2001). While processes of acculturation have been found to decrease the health advantage documented by immigrants (Lopez-Gonzalez et al. 2005), acculturation may increase the access to health care among immigrants and their families. The data presented in this current research support the idea that the immigration status of the mother does strongly affect the access to regular medical care of Hispanic children. As the duration and citizenship measures demark an "increase" in the integration of Hispanic groups into the United States (from initial duration and non-citizen all the way to ten or more years and citizen), the inequalities in access to medical care decreased (Durden and Hummer 2006).

In the final model, access to a regular source of care for the child sample did not overwhelmingly contrast between the race/ethnic subgroups of interest. Only Mexican American children are significantly different from the reference, as they are less likely to report access to a regular source of care in comparison to non-Hispanic whites. The continued disparities between Mexican American and non-Hispanic white children in reporting access to a regular source of care are significant. In spite of *all* variables being taken into account, Mexican Americans were still 36% less likely to report a usual access to health care in comparison to non-Hispanic whites. The circular migration of Mexican Americans (Massey et al. 1987; Bean et al. 2001), as well as the possible use of health care in Mexico, may facilitate this continued disparity in accessing health care within the United States (Durden and Hummer 2006).

This research contributes to the growing literature that documents health care disparities among race/ethnic minorities and the impact of immigration status on those inequalities. As the child population of the Hispanic population of the United States continues to grow relatively rapidly, policymakers will need to ensure that these children have access to the health care system. Moreover, there is a growing recognition that all children, regardless of ethnicity, should be provided with quality health care, not only for the health of the children and their families, but the health of our entire society.[1]

NOTES

1. Thanks much to Robert Hummer, Abby Miller, Marc Musick, Parker Frisbie, and Yolanda Padilla for their helpful comments.

REFERENCES

Beall, F. D. et al. 2001. Circular, invisible, and ambiguous migrants: Components of difference in estimates of the number of unauthorized Mexican migrants in the United States. *Demography* 38:411–22.

Durden, T. E. 2007. The effects of immigration on the usual source of health care among Hispanic children. Forthcoming *Medical Care*.

Durden, T. E., and R. A. Hummer. 2006. Acess to health care among working-aged Hispanics in the United States. *Social Science Quarterly* 87(5):395–419.

Flores, G. et al. 1999. The impact of ethnicity, family income, and parental education on children's health and use of health services. *American Journal of Public Health* 89(7):1066–71.

Frisbie, P. et al. 2001. Immigration and the Health of Asian and Pacific islander adults in the US. *American Journal of Epidemiology* 153:372–80.

Guendelman, S., and T. Wagner. 2000. Health Services utilization among Latinos and white non-Latinos: Results from a national survey. *Journal of Health Care for the Poor and Underserved* 11(2):179–94.

Jang M. et al. 1998. Income, language, and citizenship status: Factors affecting the health care access and utilization of Chinese Americans. *Health and Social Work* 23:136–45.

LeClere, F. et al. 1994. Health care utilization, family context and adaptation among immigrants to the United States, *Journal of Health and Social Behavior* 35:370–84.

Lieu, T. et al. 1993. Race, ethnicity, and access to ambulatory care among US adolescents. *American Journal of Public Health* 83:960–65.

Lopez-Gonzalez, L. et al. 2005. Immigrant acculturation, gender and health behavior: A research note. *Social Forces* 84(1):581–93.

Massey, D. S., R. Alarcón, H. González, and J. Durand. 1987. *Return to Aztlan: The Social Process of International Migration from Western Mexico*. Berkeley and Los Angeles: University of California Press.

Mirowsky, J. 1999. Analyzing associations between mental health and social circumstances. In *Handbook of the Sociology of Mental Health*. Ed. J. C. Phelan. New York, Kluwer Academic/Plenum Publishers. Pp. 105–23.

Novello, A. et al. 1991. Hispanic health: Time for data, time for action. *JAMA, the Journal of the Medical Association* 265(2):253–55.

Scott, G., and H. Ni 2004. *Access to Health Care Among Hispanic/Latino Children: United States, 1998–2001*. Hyattsville MD: National Center for Health Statistics.

Shetterly, S. et al. 1996. Self-rated health among Hispanic vs non-Hispanic adults: The San Luis Valley health and aging study. *American Journal of Public Health* 86:1798–1801.

Thamer, M. et al. 1997. Health insurance coverage among foreign-born US residents: The impact of race, ethnicity, and length of residence. *American Journal of Public Health* 97:96–102.

Weigers, M. et al. 1998. Children's health insurance, access to care, and health status: New findings. *Health Affairs* 17:127–36.

Weinick, R., and N. A. Krauss. 2000. Racial/ethnic differences in children's access to care. *American Journal of Public Health* 90(11):1771–74.

Weinick, R. et al. 2000. Racial and ethnic differences in access to and use of health care services, 1977–1996. *Medical Care Research and Review* 57:36–54.

Zuvekas S. H., and R. Weinick. 1999. Changes in access to care, 1977–1996: The role of health insurance. *Health Services Research* 34(1):271–79.

Botánicas in America's Backyard: Uncovering the World of Latino Healers' Herb-healing Practices in New York City

Anahí Viladrich

INTRODUCTION

Wherever you see a little bit of herbs, there you will find a remedy.

From El Monte, Cabrera 1983:83
(author's translation)

They (Latinos) are the ones who come here the most, and they are the ones that more or less share the same customs, no matter where they are from. Do you understand? We have almost the same problems, and we are Latinos, we understand each other much better . . . and that's why. . . . We are Latinos!

Diogenes, male Santeria practitioner

Previous studies on the role of botánicas (religious-healing stores) have highlighted the existence of blossoming markets of healing in the United States, particularly with regard to Latinos' use of herbs and plants to treat a variety of physical and emotional ailments (see Polk 2004; Long 2001; Delgado and Santiago 1998). Innovative research has provided a unique contribution to our understanding of immigrants' folk-healing beliefs and practices, particularly for the handling of women's health conditions (see Reiff 2003; Balick et al. 2000). In addition, the increasing interest in the farming, circulation, and use of herbs and plants in cosmopolitan milieus has been supported by the globalization of

Anahí Viladrich: "Botánicas in America's Backyard: Uncovering the World of Latino Healers' Herb-healing Practices in New York City," first published in *Human Organization*, vol. 65, num. 4 (2006): 407–19.

former syncretic traditions, brought together by the amalgam of diverse healing systems across rural and urban areas (see Vandebroek et al. 2004; Romberg 2003). This is particularly relevant in the case of Latino immigrants who, once in the United States, tend to adapt their practices to what is both available and affordable in combination with the new knowledge they gain from their exposure to multicultural contexts, particularly in cities like New York, Los Angeles, and San Francisco (Viladrich 2006). It is precisely in these cities where botánicas have become the main suppliers of plants and herbs, offering specimens that are either locally produced or brought from Miami, the Caribbean, and South America (Ososki et al. 2002, Balick et al. 2000).

New York City (NYC) offers a unique cosmopolitan milieu for the study of immigrants' use of herbs and plants, particularly given the thriving religious concoctions drawn from diverse cultures and belief systems, from voodoo among Haitians (McCarthy Brown 1991) to Santeria among Cuban-Americans (Pasquali 1994). Studies of African religious systems have been pivotal in our understanding of spiritual practices as models of resistance and accommodation towards oppression (Singer and Baer 1995; Baer and Singer 1993), and in the construction of diaspora communities in the United States (see Fernández Olmos and Paravisini-Gebert 2003; Moreno Vega 2000; McCarthy Brown 1991; Gonzalez-Whippler 1989). Herbs are intrinsic to complex religious belief systems, as in the case of African-religious traditions (e.g., Spiritism, Santeria, and Palo Monte), which combine ritual celebrations with the medicinal use of herbs and plants for different purposes (Brandon 1991; Cabrera 1971).[1] Nevertheless, and despite the growing interest in Yoruba and Congolese healing beliefs, little attention has been paid to indigenous understandings of efficacy that vary across folk-healing disciplines (Waldram 2000). A paucity of research also exists on the cultural belief systems underlying plant selection, preparation, and use, including herbs consumed for religious and magical purposes (see Factor-Litvak et al. 2001; Cushman et al. 1999). Although the conspicuous presence of Latino healers in NYC has been addressed in the literature (see Reiff et al. 2003; Balick et al. 2000; Garrison 1977) still little is known about the importance of their multi-level practices vis-à-vis their growing Spanish-speaking clientele in NYC. Health costs and lack of health insurance are paramount barriers that keep Latinos from accessing formal health care, and curanderos and other folk practitioners are still a main resource that help them solve their more pressing health needs (see Viladrich 2006; Jones et al. 2001; Baer 2001; Gomez-Beloz and Chavez 2001, Balick and Lee 2001; Velez-Ibañez and Parra 1999). Research on the role of Latino healers in assisting immigrants to solve their health ailments in urban milieus allows a better assessment of the services they provide vis-à-vis their clients' unmet needs.

This article begins by introducing the presence of botánicas as "natural sites" for the study of herbs and plants, and as a main staple for Latinos' informal economy of healing. I explore two aspects in particular, beginning with the role of botánicas as unique outlets for the access to herbal specimens, and subsequently discussing their importance as *therapeutic spaces* where Latino healers either provide consultations or are referred to them via botánicas' salesmen. Special attention will be paid to the notion of sociosoma, a term coined to denote nosological modes of causation and treatment based on social relationships (e.g., illness due to envy), and spirits' intrusion, frequently treated through *limpias* (cleansing) for the purpose of removing surrounding negative energies. The underlying hypothesis supporting this notion is that Latino healers' conceptualization of the physical body is essentially intertwined with both the physical and the social environment that prevent, as well as sustain, the sufferer's pain (see Sheper-Hughes and Lock 1987).

Within an underlying ecological framework, I argue that healers' diagnosis and treatments are aimed at removing not only sufferers' organic symptoms but also the intangible pernicious liaisons with those, both alive and dead, who allegedly cause harm (e.g., wandering souls haunting a client's house). Rather than conforming to discrete categories, plants and herbs reveal a polifunctionality in which, according to their specific preparation and combination, are able to impact on the physical, the spiritual, and the supernatural realm for the purpose of reestablishing balance in immigrants' lives. This article will finally highlight the importance of developing conceptual models on Latinos' elaborated etiologies of health and disease, including reliance on spirituality and religiosity as a holistic and integrative system of healing.

BACKGROUND AND METHODS

Between the spring 2004 and the fall of 2005, the Latino Healers team, sponsored by the Immigration and Health Initiative at Hunter College, conducted intensive fieldwork on Latinos' folk healing practices in NYC by visiting botánicas, bodegas (Latino grocery stores), and community organizations located in Latino enclaves, such as Washington Heights and East Harlem.[2] PhD graduates and students, as well as master students of urban health and anthropology, joined the team at different times in order to participate in the several stages of the research process. The team met on a regular basis, usually once a week during the spring and the summer and once a month during the fall, for the purpose of discussing mapping strategies and research findings, as well as to share learning experiences. These meetings were also accompanied by ethnographic training seminars in which basic ethnographic skills were reviewed and practiced (e.g., mock interviews).

Fieldwork activities were organized according to prearranged plans and followed up by standardized fieldnotes. Botánicas were located via different means including phone listings (i.e., Smart Pages and Superpages) and on site visits to neighborhoods presenting large concentrations of Latinos. Team members, alone and in groups of two and three, visited Manhattan (the lower East side, Washington Heights, and East Harlem), Queens (mostly Jackson Heights), Brooklyn (particularly Bushwick), and the South Bronx. Interview notes and mapping notes were reviewed by the project director and the field coordinator and also read by other team members, as a way of improving the team's research skills while learning from each other's experiences in the field. Ethnographers collected on site information on 142 botánicas, and an additional 98 were found in phone listings. Team members also participated in Santeria rituals, (e.g., *tambores*/drumming) and private healing ceremonies. Ethnographers followed referrals from bodegas' employers, *Santeros* (Santeria

priests and their followers), and street vendors who provided leads on healers' locations. This research strategy allowed the identification of a diverse
pool of practitioners who either work at botánicas' premises or at home.
Although the fieldwork experience was undoubtedly enriching, it was
far from easy. Some practitioners were reluctant to share information with
us and often resisted volunteering information about their healing practices
(Viladrich and Gómez 2006). Persistence, reassurance of confidentiality, and
the building of rapport with potential informants were pivotal to the success of this research adventure. Healers are aware of their frequently being
portrayed as "phony" practitioners by the mainstream media, and many felt
vulnerable to the hostility they had received from outsiders in the past (see
Rasmussen 2000; Singer 1990). As happens with other folk practitioners considered ineffective by mainstream medicine (Hinojosa 2002), folk practitioners in NYC are aware of the risks and serious consequences of being held
accountable for practicing medicine without a license, as well as for selling
dangerous substances, such as mercury, to the public. These fears are even
more noticeable among Santeria followers, some of whom are afraid of being
charged for the practice of animal sacrifice, which is usually carried out during religious initiation and ritual offerings to the *Orishas* (divine beings). This
is more so among foreign-born traditional practitioners who are not allowed
to legally reside in the United States on the basis of their healing careers
(Mautino 1999).

As the study progressed, however, we were able to dissipate most of the
participants' initial fears, and it became easier for us to identify and recruit
potential candidates for in-depth interviews. The research project applied a
careful screening process that allowed the assessment of candidates' eligibility. For example, being a botánica owner does not necessarily mean being
either a plant specialist or a healer, as some owners are just "business people." Latino healers were defined as providers from Latin America (first and
second generation immigrants) who practice folk and/or traditional healing
practices for which they receive compensation (e.g., cash, goods, services). A
two-phase tape-recorded interview was conducted with eligible practitioners who agreed to participate, according to the terms approved by Hunter
College's Institutional Review Board. In order to protect the identity of study
participants, numbers and pseudonyms were used to identify them. In-depth
interviews lasting an average of two hours were conducted with 56 Latino
healers who met these criteria. Interview guides addressed healers' personal
and migratory history along with their disciplinary fields, their healing and
religious beliefs, their methods for etiology and treatment, as well as their
Latino clientele's characteristics.

Although in most cases healers came to the United States from different
countries (e.g., the Dominican Republic, Cuba, Puerto Rico, and Colombia)
and were trained in diverse healing traditions, they ascribed to a variety of
healing disciplines and counseled diverse groups of clients regardless of their
specific religious beliefs. From the sample of 56 healers, 11 called themselves
Santeros, 19 self-identified as Espiritists, and 4 shared at least these two disciplines. The remaining 22 interviewees used titles that combined different

therapeutic systems, such as herb specialists, clairvoyants, and practitioners of Palo Mayombe and reiki (see Table 1). A qualitative software package (Atlas 5.0) was used for the analysis of all collected data including fieldnotes, interview schedules, and follow-ups. SPSS and Excel were utilized for the quantitative measures and graphing of healers' sociodemographic data.[3]

BOTÁNICAS' MÉTIER AND UNPROMPTED CONNOISSEURS

Botánicas are the visible door to the invisible world of folk healing practices in NYC, as they play a key role in either providing health care products and informal health services on their premises, or in referring clients to informal and formal health care providers (Viladrich 2006; Jones et al. 2001). Botánicas are located either in areas heavily populated by Latinos, or in neighborhoods currently experiencing ethnic transition marked by increasing gentrification.

To the eyes of an amateur, most botánicas' interiors may appear as esoteric bazaars, where religious icons from multiple traditions are piled up in apparent disarray amidst a cornucopia of buda and Hinduist drawings, sculptures of Catholic Saints, and Santeria necklaces. Conversely, botánicas represent a rationalized business métier in the products and the services they offer and in the social functions they play. Botánicas are unique settings that promote the informal reproduction of healing and religious networks as they welcome neighbors, patrons, healers, and salesmen who do more than business. They actually enact their belonging to religious-healing webs that lie beneath the city's informal economy of healing. As noted by Romberg (2003) botánicas are social niches that welcome religious and commercial networks where patrons and providers share knowledge about new products as well as gossip. In fact, botánicas' success greatly depends on the informal webs of those who visit them to buy and sell products, on chatting with patrons and neighbors, and on participating in religious ceremonies taking place in the religious houses and temples erected in their basements and backrooms.

By spending time at the botánicas, ethnographers were able to listen, watch, and participate in open conversations about clients' issues and about their different strategies of solving a particular problem. Healers' practice becomes then a means to make a living, while botánicas provide a place of belonging and acknowledgment among practitioners and customers seeking their help. Healing information, rather than being in the hands of just one expert, is shared and contrasted with new data that may be brought to the salesmen's and practitioners' attention. Rather than positioning themselves above their clients' status and ailments, many healers refer to stories that resonate with those brought by their clients, including having experienced traumatic migration journeys, the rupture of family bonds, and language and financial barriers. These experiences relate to what in anthropology and psychology has been designated as "the wounded healer," referring to the process by which providers connect with their own vulnerability to help others enduring similar experiences of pain, trauma, abuse, and oppression (Löyttyniemi 2005; James 2002; Dornhoefer 2001; Wolgien and Coady 1997; Sedgwick 2000).

Learning and sharing herb-related information constitutes an ongoing "oral tale" through which botánicas' owners and patrons tell each other about their search for plants and reasons for specimens' selection. Exposure to the informal healing market, which finds in the botánicas a privileged hub of knowledge, provides a sounding ground for immigrants' progressive familiarity with diverse herbs, plants, and roots. Healers achieve mastery in the use of herbs through time, along with being initiated in diverse religious traditions, as Gabriela (a Cuban Santera) tells us:

> Everybody comes with something different. The Santero comes looking for herbs, comes to pick them up to solve a person's problem. If it is 'palo' (from Palo monte), they want (herbs) to solve the problems of others. They come looking for (herbs) but they don't tell you the purpose for it. Instead, the other public comes seeking for my help; there is a lot of difference. Other times they bring the recipe that another person made for them, so they come with a list and I have to give what they say, because it is another person who is treating them, not me. There are different cases coming here.

Healers are known by word of mouth and build their reputations on the basis of their clientele's esteem and popularity (see Reiff et al. 2003). Therefore, they find in the botánicas a main outlet to supply their stock as well as to publicize their practice. Practitioners' métier is characterized by the variety of disciplines they specialize in, and the flexibility by which they are able to respond to their clients' diverse needs and requests, from bringing back an estranged husband to alleviating painful arthritis symptoms. Many first learned from parents, grandparents, and mentors who taught them how to find, collect, and prepare plant infusions when they were growing up in Cuba, Puerto Rico, or in the Dominican Republic. Plant connoisseurs, however, are not necessarily represented by botánicas' owners but by their clients who, in most cases, had used herbs in their countries of origin to treat a variety of conditions. Not all botánicas' owners are either healers or herb specialists. Therefore, they often hire folk practitioners to work on their premises.

Although not all study participants worked with herbs, most of them mentioned having learned about them in their countries of origin or from colleagues and clients in NYC. Nevertheless, when asked about the source of their knowledge, many referred to a "calling," a kind of intuitive (and metaphysical) ability that accompanied them all their life, and which was passed down to them from their ancestors. Some mentioned a sort of resistance to this calling at some point in their lives, which kept them from acknowledging their innate powers. Typically, an unexpected enlightening episode (e.g., a mentor who guided them, a sudden crisis in their lives) made them aware of their healing faculties at some point in time. In addition, using herbs does not necessarily mean that practitioners know about their properties *per se*. This is the case among those whose prescriptive knowledge comes from spirits or guardian angels who lead them, and for whom herb use is aimed at healing the spiritual and the social realm (Singer and Garcia 1989). In this study we found individuals who, in spite of sharing the same alternative healing

TABLE 1
Healers' Characteristics

Name	Gender	Country of Origin	Age	Education	Main Healing Practices
Octavio	Male	Puerto Rico	52	No Formal Education	Santero/a
Magdalena	Female	Colombia	53	Primary/Elementary	Santero/a+Espiritista
Cristobal	Male	Puerto Rico	23	High School	Santero/a
Taurel	Male	Puerto Rico	57	Some High School	Palero-Espiritista
Pino	Male	Dominican Republic	31	Some High School	Espiritista
Marieclaire	Female	Dominican Republic	50	N/A	Espiritista
Felipe	Male	Dominican Republic	30	Some College	Santero/a
Ori	Male	Puerto Rico	56	Technical High School	Espiritista
Laurina	Female	US	50	Some College	Herbalist Holistic Healer
Mariano	Male	US	26	Associate Degree	Santero/a
Gabriela	Female	Cuba	71	No Formal Education	Santero/a
Daila	Female	US	47	Some High School	Santero/a
Aristides	Male	Trinidad	37	Some College	Santero/a
Dafne	Female	Cuba	52	College	Espiritista
Leonelidas	Male	Puerto Rico	77	Primary/Elementary	Espiritista
Tea	Female	Dominican Republic	47	Primary/Elementary	Espiritista
Blanche	Female	Dominican Republic	38	Primary/Elementary	Espiritista
Narcisa	Female	Dominican Republic	38	College	Vidente/Espiritista
Artemisia	Female	Dominican Republic	50	Primary/Elementary	Espiritista
Soledad	Female	Dominican Republic	50	College	Vidente
Larisa	Female	Dominican Republic	30	Some High School	Clarividente
Ariana	Female	Peru	47	Some College	Vidente+Astrologist
Diogenes	Male	Cuba	63	College	Santero/a
Yolanda	Female	Dominican Republic	57	Some College	Espiritista
Zaida	Female	Dominican Republic	50	N/A	Espiritista
Nereida	Female	Dominican Republic	40	N/A	Sales Person at Botánica

Name	Gender	Country	Age	Education	Role
Chloe	Female	US	34	High School	Espiritista
Sigfrido	Male	Dominican Republic	26	High School	Espiritista
Carmelo	Male	Dominican Republic	38	Some High School	Espiritista
Benencio	Male	Puerto Rico	65	Junior High	Espiritista
Nuria	Female	US	31	College	Naturalistic/Holistic Medicine
Isidoro	Male	US	30	Some High School	Santero/a
Larimar	Female	Dominican Republic	48	College	Herberia
Guido	Male	Guatemala	41	Some College	Santero/a+Espiritista
Angeles	Female	Puerto Rico	57	High School	Herberia
Piero	Male	Colombia	38	Some College	Espiritista
Jacinto	Male	Colombia	53	Some College	Santero-Palero-Reiki
Ruperto	Male	Ecuador	41	N/A	Curanderismo+Naturista
Rubi	Female	Dominican Republic	74	N/A	Vidente
Azara	Female	Uruguay	37	College	Spiritual Guide
Carmelo	Male	Argentina	33	High School	Vidente
Rosenda	Female	Dominican Republic	44	N/A	Espiritista
Monique	Female	US	45	High School	Santero/a+Espiritista and Wicca
Catalina	Female	Dominican Republic	50	Some College	Espiritista
Ramiro	Male	Puerto Rico	55	College	Santero/a+Espiritista
Dario	Male	Puerto Rico	N/A	Masters	Santero/a
Soledad	Female	Puerto Rico	70	High School	Espiritista and Curanderismo
Roman	Male	Dominican Republic	64	Primary/Elementary	Espiritista
Anastasio	Male	Puerto Rico	52	High School	Santero/a+Espiritista
Solana	Female	Dominican Republic	56	Primary/Elementary	Espiritista
Timoteo	Male	Cuba	59	Primary/Elementary	Babalao/Palero
Amatista	Female	Dominican Republic	21	High School	Santero/a
Perseo Clarividente	Male	Cuba	52	Primary/Elementary	Palero-Espiritista and Santero/a and
Azucena	Female	Dominican Republic	43	High School	Spiritual Guide and Reiki
Maximo	Male	Venezuela	N/A	N/A	Consultor de Salud Natural
Carina	Female	Dominican Republic	47	N/A	Herberia

market, held different levels of spiritual and healing expertise based on their access to information, specialization, and personal experience. For example, Sigfrido, a young male spiritist from the Dominican Republic with limited knowledge about herbs and plants, regularly prescribed standard baths with herbs for the purpose of curing his clients' spiritual paths, a treatment that would gradually ease physical symptoms that included sleeplessness, anxiousness, and lack of appetite as in the case of those suffering from marital or financial problems. Most of Sigfrido's knowledge about herbs had been gained by word of mouth, both in his country of origin and from hanging out in one particular bótanica located in Washington Heights, where he eventually began to treat clients. Through time, healers like Sigfrido have become familiar with herbs and plant use as a result of their exposure to the unique opportunities offered by the eclectic NYC economy of healing.

HEALING WITH HERBS IN THE URBAN MILIEU

> There are herbs for everything. That's where it starts. From the herbs you get the powders, the sprinkling powders. You get the oils, you get the incenses. Everything starts with the plants.
>
> Aristides, male practitioner of Santeria

Herbs are mostly used in three forms: baths, teas, and in rubbing substances, such as oils. A general distinction between herbs is supported by the dichotomy between sweet and bitter ones. Sweet herbs are commonly aromatic, agreeable to the palate, and consumed as teas due to their assumed curative properties. Herbs used in infusions are mostly aimed at treating physical and organic illnesses (e.g., stomach pain, respiratory problems) as well as mental stress, as in the case of valerian and *tilo* (linden—Mazur 1995). Among sweet herbs, healers mention *romero* (rosemary), *yerbabuena* (spearmint), *albahaca* (basil), *mejorana* (marjoram), *yerbaluisa* (lemon grass), and *sabila* (aloe vera).

Bitter herbs are strong, both in smell and taste, and are more often used in baths for the purpose of changing clients' misfortune as well as to influence interpersonal domains, including repairing stressed family relationships, finding jobs, attracting good luck, and bringing back estranged lovers. Nevertheless, bitter plants may be occasionally used in infusions and vice versa. For example *anamú* (known as the ginseng of the tropics) although considered a bitter plant, is commonly used in drinkable form to cure arthritis, as well as in painful conditions of the joints due to its anti-inflammatory and analgesic properties. In the words of Artemisa (a female Espiritista from the Dominican Republic): "the drink is very bad, but they put the roots in the gin, and leave it there for it to take all the extract, because it takes all the compound, and they have to drink a little bit of it every day."

The herbs that are sold in NYC come from various sources, but primarily arrive from Miami, the Dominican Republic, Puerto Rico, and increasingly from Mexico, Brazil, and Central America. They are also grow well in the tri-state area (the states of New York, New Jersey, and Connecticut), where they are often produced on family farms. The issue of access and distribution is crucial in a milieu where plants and herbs are not usually grown in people's backyards. Healers mention difficulties in finding specific herbs at particular seasons, either because of natural disasters in the herbs' places of origin, speculation that leads to a rise in prices, or because of higher demand, particularly during the holiday months. Botánicas may not have all the plants needed and differences in presentation and form (e.g., dried, mixed, fresh) create difficulties for their identification (Ososki et al. 2002; Balick et al. 2000). Clients may visit botánicas to look for plants that are either unknown to owners and employers, or that have not previously been used in the United States (Viladrich in press, b).

Although most healers expressed their preference for fresh herbs, consumption of dried herbs and plants is widespread, partially due to the difficulties of growing them in urban areas and botánicas' limited fresh stock. With the exception of a few botánicas that specialize in fresh items, and a few healers who have access to community gardens or grow herbs themselves, most of our interviewees combine different types of herbs and plants. In some cases the healer prescribes the herbs to clients who buy them at the botánicas, but in others the practitioner buys the herbs and prepares a concoction to be used by her/his clients in the form of baths, sprays, or rubbing formula. In terms of prescriptions, some healers prefer to recommend prepackaged herbs and preparations, while others more frequently customize their recipes by prescribing herbs and oils that are mixed and prepared by their clients at home.

In addition, although botánicas continue to be the main outlet for herbs and plants, not all healers are botánicas' fans. Those who work on their own (and are not tied to any specific botánicas) are particularly suspicious about the quality and origin of botánicas' herbs, including prepackaged compounds that are regarded as *best sellers* when it comes to potions for love, luck, and money. Some express their discontent with the commercialization of herbs, which, in the past, were easily found in the *monte* (forest), public parks, and vacant lots. As Magdalena, a *Santera* and *Espiritista* from Colombia who mostly works at home, states:

> Now they are charging you even for the smile. Years ago you would go to el monte (forest) to pick the herb up, which now you have to buy. Why? Because you would tell people: "Go to that place, go and get the herb . . ." Because herbs are productive and curative there; you pick them up and you will get well.

Even if healers continue to use the plants they are familiar with, it is often difficult to follow traditional methods of collection, such as picking them in the morning or under a full moon. In addition, changes in prices may threaten the access and availability of herbs and plants. For example, the 2004 summer hurricane season affected the production, quality, and quantity of items brought from Miami. Therefore prices of many herbs increased and some botánicas experienced difficulties in trying to obtain certain herbs, as diversity and quantity of specimens were limited. In the end, botánica owners had to settle for what the distributor could provide for them. During fieldwork, our team witnessed more than one situation when botánicas' salesmen had to tell a client that a certain plant was not available but that another could have a similar effect, which reminded us of doctors when they change patients medicine around any time their preferred ones are either too expensive or no longer available.

BOTÁNICAS' BACK ROOM:
THE REALM OF THE THERAPEUTIC ENCOUNTER

Most botánicas keep a room either in the back of the store or in the basement for *consultas* (consultations) during which a healer, usually the botánica's employee or its owner, provides readings generally to one client at a time. Some botánicas work on a first-come first-serve basis while others make appointments on request. Consultas are usually for-money transactions with prices oscillating between twenty-five dollars and several hundreds. These sessions are aimed at providing clients with emotional strength and social support regarding financial and family problems as well as with life-threatening conditions, such as cancer and AIDS.[4] Practitioners usually perform as *curanderos*, diviners, religious priests, and informal mental health providers all at once, by listening and providing advice about a myriad of personal and family matters. Without forms to fill out, identification cards to present, or long waiting times to get an appointment, immigrants easily get into street-level botánicas seeking expedited responses to a pressing physical or emotional issue. As Davis (1997) observes, the act of cure through herbs is not as relevant as the act of "caring" that healers impart, and which provide a more holistic meaning to their herb-therapy treatments (e.g., preparation, application, follow up).

Asked about the reasons for consultation, most healers indicate their clients' stressful living circumstances, family and marital issues (e.g., domestic violence, infidelity), health problems, *nervios* (nerves) and other mental conditions, such as depression. Healers customarily prescribe herbs to help their clients deal with any of the above ailments. The most challenging aspect of a provider's job is to locate the source of their clients' suffering, which may require diverse diagnostic procedures. Clients' problems may be organic or psychological in nature, or due to spiritual disturbances and *trabajos* (witchcraft) ordered by either former lovers or jealous relatives. Diagnosis is usually sought via divination (e.g., tarot, aura reading, crystals), through consultation with the pantheon of Orishas, or with the healer's protective spirits, as stated by Daila, a female Santera:

> Yeah, you do a consulta . . . it depends on what the problem is and it depends on what your spirit guides send you. . . . Cause you're really in semi-trance there. . . . When you're doing a consulta you're in a basic semi-trance because you're having the communion with your spirits. And egún, which is people's dead ancestor, will exactly direct you to what it is that this specific person needs.

Healers distinguish between an evil caused by others and organic or psychologically inflicted trauma. These distinctions are assessed through visions they have during consultations, readings they make from their clients' aura (electromagnetic field), or the ongoing assistance they receive from spirits or divinities (e.g., *Orishas* in Santeria religion) that inform them about the nature of their clients' problems. Mariano, a male santero of Latino origin, tells us:

> A card reading, correct. Just to see the overall life. And then there's this process. . . . Like a scanning where I scan from head to toe to see the areas of the body that the person has to be careful with. . . . When I'm talking to the person after I've done the general reading about their life and all the material things, then I go through the health and I describe all the things to them. Some cards will identify heart, lungs, and liver. . . . But other things, like, I'll feel them. Like I'll scan a person's body and I'll feel like this nervousness or like a fear, it's like a fear, like a nervous feeling. When I'm thinking of a certain part of the body, then that means that that area is going to be affected.

Healers may use different methods to read a client's soul, energy, or aura, which are aimed at interpreting the waves transmitted by a person's underlying energy. For example Marco, a male Colombian spiritist, explains:

> People who read the tongue, the eyes, the candle, the glass of water. . . . Perhaps that doesn't exist, what exists is the connection with the aura. So someone tells you they are going to read the aura to you, the iris, and they tell you: "You will have a trip". Another person looks at the glass of water and tells you: "Oh, you will have a trip." But it is not that they are reading the candle or the glass of water. It is that they are using that element to soften the energy, to control the energy. . . . They are actually working on the person's aura.

The ability to etiologically distinguish between the natural and the supernatural causes of clients' disorders is at the bottom of healers' expertise, usually determined by the issues brought to the *consulta*. Healers emphatically mention the need to make a distinction between the physical, the mental, the spiritual, and the magical realm as the first step towards providing an accurate diagnosis of a client's real ailments. Nevertheless, these differences are in practice not as conclusive since organic problems, such as headaches or repetitive vomiting, may be triggered by either spiritual or energetic sources. Ambiguity and imprecision is also at the basis of healers' assessments of efficacy. As noted by Waldram (2000), efficacy in traditional medicine is still an elusive concept: not only is it subjected to shifting consensus, but it also depends on the specific criteria applied by those who are both insiders and outsiders of the healing process, including providers, their patients, and the community at large (Kleinman 1980; Kleinman and Sung 1979).

Given the fact that folk healers rely on indicators that are mostly non-biomedical, it is not always easy to identify the criteria assumed by diverse healing paradigms to assess their results and impact. For example, when asked about their own assessment of effectiveness, participants were likely to refer to successful cases they treated, as well as to the prestigious reputation they held against their competitors. In fact, most participants were eager to mention the incompetence of many of their colleagues, while seeming often evasive in assessing the basis of their own achievements besides boasting about the many cases they "cured" once and for all. This manifestation of success relates to two complementary aspects in the conceptualization of efficacy. First, as healers' gold standards are not systematized on the basis of either professional protocols or external evaluation, there is no clear way to validate standard practices besides practitioners' own assessment of success. Second, given the competitive market of healing in NYC, having a well-supplied botánica and a waiting room crowded with customers become the ultimate proof that their methods work. As first suggested by Lévi-Strauss (1963), healers' position of prestige often becomes the basis from which their assumed healing skills are then taken at face value.

In terms of concrete indicators, healers' notions of efficacy cover a wide range depending on the problem treated. Among our study participants, when the issue was directly linked to physical health, efficacy was more likely seen as an organic or a physical outcome such as removing most of the symptoms of, for example, chronic arthritis pain or asthma attacks. When discussing these cases, some practitioners claimed their healing superiority over medicine, which they considered more dangerous due to its emphasis on chemicals, the use of surgery and other invasive treatments, and the preeminence of a for-profit ethos. Indeed, most healers privileged the use of herbs over pharmaceuticals particularly for minor conditions, as they often considered the latter a symptom of the pecuniary aims of the health industry over patients' best interests. When explaining the natural antibiotic properties of plants such as *sabia* (aloe vera) and *maravilla* (calendula), interviewee Daila, a female Santera, stated:

> So instead of going out and buying Neosporin you go out and buy a little of each plant, you take it, you boil it, you take the plant out, you put it in a mortar, you know, uh! You put a little drop of oil, so that it's a lubricant . . . and you put it on this little child' bruise or scrape or whatever and it goes away; and now you've not put chemicals on your kid.
>
> The Latinos believe that too . . . that the Western people, the American people they don't want to cure you. Why bother finding a cure? When . . . where your money is—is in your pharmaceuticals. And half those pharmaceuticals they sell us are synthetic with horrendous side effects. Gee, great! Now you are going to fix my blood pressure but my liver is going to go. . . . So what?

Nevertheless, less conclusive notions of efficacy seem to be at stake when dealing with conditions related to the intervention of the spiritual and the social world (sociosoma). As it will be further explained in the next section, whenever the root of the problem was attributed to either *trabajos* (spells and sorcery) or spirits' intrusion, efficacy was more likely to be assessed as an enduring process that would involve fixing the social and the spiritual environment (see Waldram 2000; Finkler 1994). To a certain extent, Spiritists and Santeros become the embodiment on earth of the divinities in heaven, with the gift to translate divine wishes to help clients with love, health, and work

matters. Hence, healers' therapeutic packages often combine diverse procedures that include praying, lighting of *velones* (candles), baths, and religious
rituals.

SOCIOSOMA: THE ECOLOGICAL FRAMEWORK
OF THE HEALING ENCOUNTER

For most healers, natural and supernatural causes are interconnected, as the
organic body conveys individual emotions as well as the surrounding energies from both the living and the dead. Conditions that may be rooted in
natural causes may have supernatural symptoms and vice-versa. As previously discussed, due to the changeability among the mental, the emotional,
and the spiritual realm, healers argue that many health conditions may origi-
nate in social forces, including spells sent to a client by an envious relative or
surrounding negative energies drawn from a recently deceased co-worker.
In addition, spirits display dual characters in terms of their ability to heal
and harm. For instance "angels" or "guides" may guide a medium on how to
release a person's soul or do just the opposite. A reckless spirit may be drawn
to a person's aura by creating visions, nightmares, and dual perceptions of
reality. In the words of Octavio:

> I see the spirit side during the consultation, I can see if a person really did what
> it is blamed for or if he is innocent. . . . But (in some cases) hey! They send you
> a reckless spirit, a desperate spirit to do everything for things to go bad. It is
> because of all the problems that the spirit is bringing to you, the reason why you
> will kill yourself. It is not because the person is going to kill you directly; it is the
> envy, the evilness. . . . And you get desperate: you break up your marriage, you
> get fired, the credit cards are on top of you, your children get sick. . . . This is the
> system that alters the person's nerves, so the same person acts out to take her
> life away. . . . In some cases they end up in the 'manicomio' (psychiatric facility),
> which is full with cases like this one.

Healers' intervention via ritualistic cleansing plays an important role in
the resolution of their Latino clients' ailments, whose etiology is rooted in
sociosoma disturbances rather than in psychosomatic indicators (Viladrich
2006). Sociosoma refers to modes of causation that are based on social relationships (e.g., illness due to envy), the intrusion of unwelcome spirits, as
well as those related to distressful social and living circumstances (e.g., financial hardships, immigrants' undocumented status). The notion of sociosoma
draws its features from diverse cultural belief systems (e.g., Santeria, Spiritism, Palo Mayombe) that share an explanatory model of disease (Kleinman
1980; Sandoval 1979), which posits the inter-connectedness of the individual
ego with the physical and social environment. Therefore, rather than fixing
the external world, healers attempt to mend the severed linkages among those
inhabiting it. No longer understood as the dyadic combination of mind versus
body, human beings are tied to others through intangible fields of energy
(Wedel 1999; Sheper-Hughes and Lock 1987; Brown 1988). During fieldwork,

healers shared with us stories of clients falling sick in places haunted by evil spirits. Even if witchcraft was not focused on a particular person, those who were younger or weaker seemed more susceptible to its effects.

The healing process therefore implies acknowledging the fluidity between the self and others, as well as accepting one's vulnerability to harmful energies more often fed by friends and relatives' envy, jealousy, and possessive behavior as well as wandering spirits looking for a host (see Koss-Chioino 1992; Harwood 1977a and 1977b). It is precisely because of the insidious character attributed to many drifting spirits that healers warn their godchildren and clients to protect themselves from unsolicited advice or possession, a common problem among inexperienced apprentices (Turner 2005).[5] Tea, a Dominican woman who self-defined as a spiritist, reported:

> Like with a lady who went to a wake and the spirit took over her. . . . And he didn't let her sleep, she had swollen eyes you know . . . because she couldn't sleep, work, eat and many more things and she was nervous. . . . So she went to the doctor. . . . The doctor didn't find anything; everything continued to be the same. . . . So somebody told her to come here, so I began treating her until she got cured all at once. . . . I told her that this wasn't related to any medicine or doctor, that that was something between God and me.

SOCIOSOMA IN ACTION: THE POWER OF LIMPIAS AND BATHS

> Plants are for different purposes. There are plants used to "limpiar el mal" (remove evil), there are plants that have curative power, and there are plants that are to attract good luck, I mean positive plants, and this depends on how the plant is used.
>
> Angeles, female herbist

All across Latin America, *limpias* (cleansing) are well-known procedures for treatment, for which rubbing plants and produce (e.g., eggs, coconuts) and herbal drinks are common (Laguerre 1987). Particularly within Afro-Caribbean healing traditions, there exists the belief that the body's internal filth causes several maladies, which also translates into the impurity of the blood (Brandon 1991). Among Latino practitioners to cleanse means to purify, heal, and relieve both body and soul from bad influences while attracting positive ones. Limpias are generally used to purify three domains: body, spirit, and the surrounding physical and social environment by relying on herbs mixed with diverse substances and specimens such as fruits, alcohol, and honey. The act of purifying the body is emphatically associated with cleaning the soul, the spirit and the aura (Viladrich 2005).

For example, Leonelidas, a male Espiritista from Puerto Rico, explains that the best way to relieve oneself from kidney problems is to decontaminate the system with *cocidos* of herbs (cooked herbs), for which different specimens are prepared either separately or combined. The use of mixed herbs is a common practice particularly in the case of inflammatory conditions (arthritis), for which *anamú* and ginger, *cola de caballo* (horsetail), and *palo de Brazil* (Brazil bark) are typically used. Certainly, limpias are the most conspicuous form of treatment, not only encompassing the individual body but also its surrounding milieu. As noted earlier, cleansing exceeds the individual self and taps into clients' external environment. Having a limpia done in someone's home becomes a metaphor for fixing stressed social relationships, for easing the path towards success, for assuring physical recovery, or for reconciliation in the case of strained family relationships. Diogenes, a male *babalao* (highest priest), practitioner of Santeria and Palo Mayombe, prescribes different fruits, vegetables, and plants to distil the inner body as well as its external environment. For example, he mentioned having garlic smashed with sugar, olive oil, and bits to clean the body, including intestines, and colic pain. He also uses *álamo* (poplar) for external cleansing that clears the air for other herbs, such as basil:

> The difference is that basil is used after the cleansing, the cleansing is with álamo that gathers any negative thing that is lingering in the house. So then I get the basil plant, which is natural, that smells very nicely, and I place it there to refresh (the client's house).

Healers typically recommend spiritual cleansing by combining water, ammonia, and camphor that are put in a glass bowl in each of the four corners of one's house to get rid of negative energies. Camphor and alcohol are also used to mop the floor and to purify both the soul and the environment due to their calming effect, their refreshing smell, and their disinfectant properties. Artemisa, a female spiritist from the Dominican Republic, provides a clear example of the financial stressors experienced by her clients, and the importance of decontaminating the physical environment to assure that positive energies, as well as good business, will pass through a client's door:

> This boy (who had a business) the day before yesterday came with the problem that he wasn't working, he was not doing business, and I told him: "At least once in a while you should clean yourself up: throw blue (indigo) and camphor by the door and that will clean the door in the morning." Sometimes, when not many people enter the store, you have to clear the entry door up at least with something.

Baths are probably the most popular form of cleansing, besides infusions, which are mostly applied to repel bad luck and break the negative path, as in the case of *despojos* and *rompimientos*. *Despojos* is a type of cleansing ritual used to liberate a person from harmful spirits and evil spells, for which botánicas offer the Seven African Powers, rompezaraguey and Saint Michael (see Gonzalez-Wippler 1989). *Rompimientos* are meant to break down the linkages between a person and surrounding negative energies and are also accomplished by using special baths. When prescribing baths, healers mix flowers and herbs with scents, oils, and rose petals in tubs of water in which clients bathe starting from the head downward, a procedure that is often repeated for between three and seven days. A bath aimed at bringing good luck will combine rue, blessed water, basil, pepper, mint, patchouli, sesame, rice, and corn. Sweet baths are aimed at attracting love, jobs, and money, and usually combine boiled flowers, such as roses from different colors and varieties, cinnamon (considered an aphrodisiac) and sweet clover. Narcisa, a female clairvoyant and Spiritist from the Dominican Republic and specialist in rompimientos, tells us that she prepares herbal baths "with my own hands because my hands are blessed," for which she uses flowers, oils, and perfumes. Nevertheless she is quick to point out that using the right herbs and plants does not necessarily guarantee a successful outcome, as it is the spiritual power that imprints the strength on the natural elements. In her own words: "Everything is guided by the spirit. . . . It's another ritual that I actually do to give light to that entity. . . . To guide that spirit out through prayers. You lead that spirit to its resting place through prayers."

In addition, although most botánicas do not openly advertise Santeria services, it is easy to recognize the influence of Santeria in the products they sell, including bead necklaces (fundamental pieces in Santeria's reliquaries) and sprays and soaps named after the Siete Potencias Africanas (Seven African Potencies) in clear reference to the seven major Orishas belonging to the Santeria pantheon. In Santeria religion, not only are herbs intrinsically able to help or harm humans, but they also hold individual character based on their inner energy or ashé. Healers who are also Santeros call attention to the connection between herbs' diverse properties and the religious powers that endow them with the ability to either cure or harm, making it difficult to distinguish their religious meaning from their medical properties. There also exists a syncretic language that connects plants to particular Orishas, for which healers attempt to become its faithful translators (Viladrich in press, b). Herbs, according to Santeria and other African-religious traditions, have intrinsic "vibrations" and metha-physical properties that attract either good or bad luck towards health, business, love, and friendship. These properties are enhanced through the combination of other elements of ritualistic practice, including successive baths accompanied by praying. Guido, a male Santero and Espiritista from Guatemala, argues:

> All herbs have certain properties, properties that you have to study, for finances, for business, for harmony in your aura, in love issues, for protection against enemies. So, a specific herb combination will produce a vibration, and if you apply it in the right way that vibration will become part of your aura—when you get into the water with the herbs, and from that point it will surround you and will give you a kind of protection.

Healers are also aware of their Latino clients struggle with conditions in the city, which have an impact on both their physical and emotional health (Trotter and Chavira 1981). For that reason, most intervene in their clients' everyday tribulations, by offering them a space where religion and magic are intertwined with practical philosophy. Gabriela, for example, uses the term cleansing in a literal meaning to refer to her clients' "cleaning" of their physical space: "The house has to be clean, in the house it cannot be shoes left everywhere, old things, dirty sinks, roaches, mice. . . . People don't know that, but the cleaner you keep your apartment, the more light you have." And Guido states:

> It is not the case that you are going to have a luck bath and you will win the lotto. If someone comes with problems with immigration, it is not only with lighting a green candle that the judge will bring the papers to his home. So, one gives them information about where to call, one can recommend them centers with lawyers who won't charge them much, whom I know are not going to swindle those without money. One shows them the steps to follow, to obtain the correct information to see if they can obtain a result. . . . Or if they have working problems, because besides the spiritual side, I am going to see them physically, if they need a haircut, if they have bad breath. . . . There has to be a balance between the physical and the spiritual (realm); not only with ten baths of rue and pepper mint are you going to get a job as a congressperson!

CONCLUSIONS AND IMPLICATIONS

This article examined the role of botánicas as multilevel outlets where salesmen, healers, and customers gather to share information, participate in rituals, and buy herbs or roots to treat specific syndromes from headaches and *nervios* (nerves) to uterine fibrous, endometriosis, or hot flashes (Balick and Lee 2001; Ososki et al. 2002). As previously discussed, healers' use of herbs is embedded in an ecological framework of healing, in which the organic body is intrinsically linked to both the physical and the social environment. Although practitioners prescribe specific treatments to treat single conditions (e.g., aloe vera for asthma), they largely rely on *limpias* by combining baths with infusion of herbs in order to intervene in all dimensions of a client's life. Like looking for an organized principle behind the power of plants and herbs, healers are committed to drawing their inner properties beyond their physical, organic, and chemical attributes. As previously noted, most of the plants, herbs, and roots found at the botánicas not only have natural but also supernatural properties able to deal with the multi-dimensional aspects of disease and well being. It is herbs' *ashé*, or their divine power, that supersedes their organic and chemical compounds and that allows humans to clean their social and physical environment, as well as render tribute to the spirits and divinities that should protect them.

The notion of sociosoma underlines healers' multilevel conceptualization of plants and herbs, by referring to a cultural model in which healers consider social liaisons to account for their clients' suffering. Personhood is no longer assumed to be an individual entity, but a flowing construction in which one's self is tied to others. Herbs' importance far exceeds their proven chemical or physiological properties, as their use becomes a metaphor for strained social relationships, and as they build hope among those experiencing ongoing everyday stress.

The above findings suggest the need for more comprehensive paradigms of health and disease that encompass indigenous models of etiology, diagnosis, and treatment. Health professionals in general and mental health practitioners in particular need to be sensitive to their clients' religious, spiritual, and cultural beliefs. Sociomedical paradigms often focus on the notion of efficacy, in terms of successful/expected outcomes, mostly via measurable indicators that tend to overlook alternative forms of healing that lead to beneficial health results (Freidenberg 2000). Planning and implementing interventions that conceptualize folk beliefs and cultural practices as deviant from the American cultural norm, may lead to pathologizing ethnic groups rather than to understanding the extent to which their healing and religious practices are actually successful coping strategies in hostile social environments (Viladrich in press, a). Still, much research needs to be done, particularly regarding the effective use of herbs for medicinal and religious purposes. We also need more information about the beneficial, as well as the harmful, effect of plants in order to adjust clinical settings to immigrants' spiritual and cultural practices (Baez and Hernandez 2001). The fact that herbs and plants have different names, and are processed with other substances, creates obstacles in assessing their singular effect.[6]

Our findings about Latinos' multiple uses of herbs and plants have hopefully contributed to a better understanding of the blossoming field of indigenous healing traditions in post-industrialized societies. The ultimate goal of this paper has been to encourage integrative research models of Latinos' nosologies of herb and plant use, models that are able to account for the role of spirituality and religiosity in shaping evolving holistic systems of healing (see Cabrera 1971; Brandon 1991). Not only has plant-based healing grown in NYC in recent years, but it has also kept developing amidst multiple religious and spiritual systems. As medical pluralism tends to become the norm rather than the exception around the world (see McGrath 1999; Miles 1998; Kleinman 1980). Latino healers will probably continue adapting their practices to that which is available to them. This includes learning from both clients and colleagues, substituting new herbs and plants for those no longer available in new contexts, and combining healing methods for the purpose of creating a unique urban *herbalcopeia* (Ososki et al. 2002, 286). Herbs and plants will be here to stay, as long as they are assumed to have the power to fix not just organic maladies, but also the disrupted social environment of the most vulnerable of all.

NOTES

1. Both Santeria and Palo Monte or Palo Mayombe (usually referred as *el Palo*) belong to the African Diasporic religions and rest on the belief of divinities associated with Catholic Saints, as well as on the veneration of the spirits of the dead. Different from Santeria that has its roots in Yoruba region, *el Palo* comes from the Congo and is founded on the power of sticks (hence the word "palo," meaning "stick"). Sticks provide the force that connect followers with the spirits' powers. Many practitioners of Santeria are also followers of Palo Monte, who are known as *Paleros*.

2. Community organizations are non-profit groups, generally led by Latino entrepreneurs who sponsor cultural and artistic projects within their communities.

3. The two largest national groups represented in our sample (Dominicans and Puerto Ricans), correspond with the two dominant Latino groups in NYC (see Census Bureau 2001; The New York City Department of City Planning 2004).

4. These findings agree with others, which underscore the role of nonbiomedical practitioners to cope with illness episodes. For example, in a study with HIV-infected Hispanics in the US, Suarez et al. (1996) concluded that despite medical treatments, most participants engaged in folk healing practices, mostly spiritualism and/or Santeria, for the purpose of seeking both spiritual and physical relief, as well as protection from evil forces.

5. As noted by anthropologist Edith Turner (2005:xxiii) when referring to the realm of spiritual healing: "Spirits tend to be insistent: they take the initiative, they take one by the scruff of one's neck and deposit one in an unfamiliar vocation. They are sometimes visible, they often speak; they choose a person, and a person does not choose them."

6. The fact that plants and herbs are sold in many forms brings additional obstacles to their identification in urban markets. Healers may know the same species by different common names (see Balick et al. 2000).

REFERENCES

Baer, Hans E. 2001. *Biomedicine and Alternative Healing in America: Issues of Class, Race, Ethnicity, and Gender*. Madison: University of Wisconsin Press.

Baer, Hans A., and Merrill Singer. 1993. *African-American Religion in the Twentieth Century: Varieties of Protest and Accommodation*. Knoxville: University of Tennessee Press.

Baez, Annecy, and David Hernandez. 2001. Complementary spiritual beliefs in the Latino community: The interface with psychotherapy. *American Journal of Orthopsychiatry* 71(4):408–15.

Balick, Michael J., Fredi Kronenberg, Andreana L. Ososki, Marianne Reiff, Adriane Fugh-Berman, Bonnie O'Connor, M. Roble, P. Lohr, and D. Atha. 2000. Medicinal plants used by Latino healers for women's health conditions in New York City. *Economic Botany* 54(3):344–57.

Balick, Michael J., and Roberta Lee. 2001. Looking within: Urban ethnomedicine and ethnobotany. *Alternative Therapies* 7(4):114–15.

Brandon, George. 1991. The uses of plants in healing in an Afro-Cuban religion, santeria. *Journal of Black Studies* 22(1):55–76.

Brown, Michael Fobes. 1988. Shamanism and its discontents. *Medical Anthropology Quarterly* 2(2):102–20.

Cabrera, Lidia. 1971. *El Monte*. Miami: Colleccion Chichereku.

Cushman, Linda F., Christine Wade, Pam Factor-Litvak, Fredi Kronenberg, and L. Firester. 1999. Use of complementary and alternative medicine among African-American and Hispanic women in New York City: A pilot study. *Journal of American Medical Women's Association* 54(4):193–95.

Davis, Ruth E. 1997. Understanding ethnic women's experiences with pharmacopeia. *Health Care for Women International* 18(5):425–37.

Delgado Melvin and Jorge Santiago. 1998. HIV/AIDS in a Puerto Rican/Dominican community: A collaborative project with a botánicas shop. *Social Work* 43(2):183–86.

Dornhoefer, Joan D. 2001. Deconstructing the ailment: One health care's professional experience as the patient. *Social Work in Health Care* 33(2):105–11.

Factor-Litvak Pam, Linda F. Cushman, Fredi Kronenberg, Christine Wade, Debra Kalmuss. 2001. Use of complementary and alternative medicine among women in New York City: A pilot study. *Journal of Alternative and Complementary Medicine* 7(6)659–66.

Fernández Olmos, Margarite and Lizabeth Paravisini-Gebert. 2003. *Creole Religions of the Caribbean: An Introduction from Vodou and Santeria to Obeah and Espiritismo.* New York: New York University Press.

Finkler, Kaja. 1994. Sacred healing and biomedicine compared. *Medical Anthropology Quarterly* 8:178–97.

Freidenberg, Judith, N. 2000. *Growing Old in* El Barrio. New York and London: New York University Press.

Garrison, Vivian. 1977. Doctor, Espiritista or psychiatrist? Health seeking behavior in a Puerto Rican neighborhood of New York City. *Medical Anthropology* 1:65–191.

Gomez-Beloz, Alfredo and Noel Chavez. 2001. The *botánica* as a culturally appropriate health care option for Latinos. *The Journal of Alternative and Complementary Medicine* 7(5):537–46.

González-Wippler, Migene. 1989. *Santeria: The Religion: A Legacy of Faith, Rites, and Magic.* New York: Harmony Books.

Harwood, Alan. 1977a. *Spiritist as Needed: A Study of a Puerto Rican Community Health Resource.* New York: John Wiley and Sons.

———. 1977b. Puerto Rican spiritism. Part I—description and analysis of an alternative psychotheapeutic approach. *Culture, Medicine and Psychiatry* 1(1):69–95.

Hinojosa, Servando Z. 2002. The hands know: Bodily engagement and medical impasse in highland Maya bonesetting. *Medical Anthropology Quarterly* 16(1):22–40.

James, Allen. 2002. Reflections on Henri Nouwen's "wounded healer" as a model for contemporary social work practice. *Social Work and Christianity* 29(3):240–47.

Jones, Michael Owen and Patrick A. Polk, with Ysamur Flores-Peña and Roberta J. Evanchuk. 2001. Invisible hospitals: Botánicas in ethnic health care. In *Healing Logics: Culture and Medicine in Modern Health Belief Systems.* Erika Brady, ed. Pp. 39–87. Logan: Utah State University Press.

Kleinman, Arthur. 1980. *Patients and Healers in the Context of Culture: An Exploration of the Borderland Between Anthropology, Medicine, and Psychiatry.* Berkeley: University of California Press.

Kleinman, Arthur and L. U. Sung. 1979. Why do indigenous practitioners successfully heal? *Social Science and Medicine* 13 B(1):7–26.

Koss-Chioino, Joan D. 1992. *Women as Healers, Women as Patients: Mental Health Care and Traditional Healing in Puerto Rico.* Boulder, Colo.: Westview Press.

Laguerre, Michel. 1987. *Afro-Caribbean Folk Medicine.* South Hadley, Mass.: Bergin and Garvey.

Lévi-Strauss, Claude. 1963. The sorcerer and his magic. In *Structural Anthropology.* Pp. 163–185. New York: Basic Books.

Long, Carolyn Morrow. 2001. *Spiritual Merchants.* Knoxville: University of Tennessee Press.

Löyttyniemi, Varpu. 2005. Doctors as wounded storytellers: Embodying the physician and gendering the body. *Body and Society* 11(1):87–110.

Mautino, Kathrin S. 1999. Faith versus the law: Traditional healers and immigration. *Journal of Immigrant Health* 1(3):125–31.

McCarthy Brown, Kathleen. 1991. *Mama Lola: A Vodou Priestess in Brooklyn.* Berkeley, Los Angeles, London: University of California Press.

Miles, Ann. 1998. Science, nature, and tradition: The mass-marketing of natural medicine in urban Ecuador. *Medical Anthropology Quarterly* 12(2):206–25.

Moreno Vega, Marta. 2000. *The Altar of My Soul: The Living Traditions of Santeria.* New York: Random House.

New York City Department of City Planning. 2004. *The Newest New Yorkers 2000: Immigrant New York in the New Millennium.* New York: New York City Department of City Planning.

Ososki, Andreana L., Patricia Lohr, Marian Reiff, Michael J. Balick, Fredi Kronenberg, Adriane Fugh-Berman, Bonnie O'Connor. 2002. Ethnobotánical literature survey of medicinal plants in the Dominican Republic used for women's health conditions. *Journal of Ethnopharmacology* 79:285–98.

Pasquali, Elaine A. 1994. Santeria. *Journal of Holistic Nursing* 12(4):380–90.

Polk, Patrick Arthur. 2004. *Botánica Los Angeles: Latino Popular Religious Art in the City of Angeles.* Los Angeles: UCLA Fowler Museum of Cultural History.

Rasmussen, Susan J. 2000. Parallel and divergent landscapes: Cultural encounters in the ethnographic space of Tuareg medicine. *Medical Anthropology Quarterly* 14(2):242–70.

Reiff, Marian, Bonnie O'Connor, Fredi Kronenberg, Michael Balick, Patricia Lohr. 2003. Ethnomedicine in the urban environment: Dominican healers in New York City. *Human Organization* 61:12–26.

Risser, Amanda L., Lynette Mazur. 1995. Use of folk remedies in a Hispanic population. *Archives of Pediatrics and Adolescent Medicine* 149(9):978–81.

Romberg, Raquel. 2003. *Witchcraft and Welfare: Spiritual Capital and the Business of Magic in Modern Puerto Rico.* Austin: University of Texas Press.

Sandoval, Mercedes C. 1979. Santeria as a mental health care system: An historical overview. *Social Science and Medicine* 13B:137–51.

Sedgwick, David. 2000. The wounded healer: countertransference from a jungian perspective. Philadelphia: Brunner-Routledge.

Sheper-Hughes, Nancy and Margaret M. Lock. 1987. The mindful body: A prolegomenon to future work in medical anthropology. *Medical Anthropology Quarterly* 1(1):6–41.

Singer, Merril. 1990. Psychic surgery: Close observation of a popular healing practice. *Medical Anthropology Quarterly* 4(4):443–51.

Singer, Merril and Hans Baer. 1995. *Critical Medical Anthropology.* Amityville, N.Y.: Baywood Publishing Company.

Singer, Merrill and Roberto Garcia. 1989. Becoming a Puerto Rican espiritista: Life history of a female healer. In *Women as Healers: Cross Cultural Perspectives.* Carol Shepherd McClain, ed. Pp. 157–85. New Brunswick, N.J.: Rutgers University Press.

Suarez M., M. Raffaelli and Ann O'Leary. 1996. Use of folk healing practices by HIV-infected Hispanics living in the United States. *AIDS Care* 8(6):683–690.

Trotter, Robert T. and Juan Antonio Chavira. 1981. Mexican American folk healing. Athens: University of Georgia Press.

Turner Edith. 2005. *Among the Healers. Stories of Spiritual and Ritual Healing around the World.* Westport, Conn.: Praeger.

US Census Bureau. 2001. *The Hispanic Population Census 2000 Brief.* Washington D.C.: US Census Bureau.

Vandebroek I, P. Van Damme, L. Van Puyvelde, S. Arrazola, N. De Kimpe. 2004. A comparison of traditional healers' medicinal plant knowledge in the Bolivian Andes and Amazon. *Social Sciences and Medicine* 59(4):837–49.

Vélez-Ibañez, Carlos G. and Camilo Garcia Parra. 1999. Trauma issues and social modalities concerning mental health concepts and practices among Mexicans of the Southwest United States with reference to other Latino groups. In *Honoring Differences: Cultural Issues in the Treatment of Trauma and Loss.* Kathleen Nader and Nancy Dubrow, eds. Pp. 76–97.

Viladrich, Anahí. 2005. Can you read my aura? Latino healers in New York City. *Anthropology News* 46(2):56.

———. 2006. Beyond the supranatural: Latino healers treating Latino immigrants in New York City. *The Journal of Latino-Latin American Studies* 2(1):134–48.

———. in press, a. Latino immigrant health in the US: A growing field amidst unraveling challenges. *The Journal of Latino-Latin American Studies.* In press.

————. in press, b. Between bellyaches and lucky charms: Revealing Latinos' plant-healing knowledge in New York City. In *Travelling Plants: Ethnopharmacology, Ethnobiology and Migration.* Andrea Pieroni and Ina Vandebroek, eds. Berghahn Books. In press.

Viladrich, Anahí and Gomez, Maria. 2006. Subverting the ethnographic encounter: Role reversals and the challenge to the interviewer's role. Paper presented at the meeting of the Society for Anthropology of North America, New York City, April 20–22.

Waldram, James B. 2000. The efficacy of traditional medicine: Current theoretical and methodological issues. *Medical Anthropology Quarterly* 14(4):603–25.

Wedel, Johan. 1999. *Santeria Healing.* Gainesville: University of Florida Press.

Wolgien, Cyril S. and Nick F. Coady. 1997. Good therapists' beliefs about the development of their helping ability: The wounded healer paradigm revisited. *The Clinical Supervisor* 15(2):19–35.

"She's 16 Years-Old and There's Boys Calling Over to the House": An Exploratory Study of Sexual Socialization in Latino Families

Marcela Raffaelli and Lenna L. Ontai

INTRODUCTION

As primary agents of socialization, families play a major role in shaping developmental experiences during childhood and adolescence. Parents act as models, engage in direct and indirect teaching, attempt to mold their children's behavior in specific ways and expose their children to, or protect them from, an array of experiences (Burgental and Goodnow 1998; Parke and Buriel 1998). Although there is a rich literature showing the importance of parents in the socialization process, one aspect of socialization that has received less attention is sexual socialization.

There is widespread agreement that parents influence their children's sexual development in significant ways (for reviews, see Katchadourian 1990; Udry and Campbell 1994). Family influences on sexuality operate through a complex web of factors, including direct communication (Fox and Inazu 1980; Casper 1990; Jaccard and Dittus 1993; Holtzman and Rubinson 1995), social control practises (Miller et al. 1986), and emotional qualities of the relationship (Jaccard et al. 1998).

The exact mechanisms of influence may be unknown but ultimately family socialization affects the formation of sexual scripts, or guidelines for sexual interaction (Simon and Gagnon 1986). According to scripting theory, sexual behavior results from the interplay between cultural scenarios, interpersonal scripts and intrapsychic scripts (Simon and Gagnon 1986, 1987). Cultural scenarios provide the basic framework for sexual interactions, delineating the roles of individuals in a sexual encounter,

Marcela Raffaelli and Lenna L. Ontai: "'She's 16 Years-Old and There're Boys Calling Over to the House': An Exploratory Study of Sexual Socialization in Latino Families," first published in *Culture, Health and Sexuality*, vol. 3, num. 3 (2001): 295–310.

whereas interpersonal and intrapsychic scripts are the outcome of individual fine-tuning through experience and practice.

Scripting theory gives a prominent place to culture, which has become a central concern of developmental scholars in recent years. Culture assumes a significant role in the socialization process by shaping the specific beliefs and values held by parents (McDade 1993). Parents of ethnically diverse children face a dual socialization challenge of not only transmitting their own beliefs and values, but also those of the larger population (Parke and Buriel 1998). Thus, to gain a full understanding of sexual socialization among different ethnic groups, parents' cultural beliefs must be taken into account. The current analysis draws on a retrospective study of sexual socialization in a sample of women of Latin American origin or descent living in the US. This focus was initially prompted by the fact that US Latinas are at high risk for negative sexual outcomes.

In contrast to the general decline in sexual activity among teenagers in the USA, the proportion of Latinas of this age reporting sexual activity increased between 1988 and 1995 (from 49% to 55%) whereas contraceptive use at most recent sexual intercourse decreased (from 69% to 53%) (Child Trends 2000). In 1995, 50% of White females reported sexual activity, and 71% used contraception at last intercourse; 60% of Black females were sexually active, with 70% reporting contraceptive use. Given these ethnic disparities, it is perhaps not surprising that in 1997 the teen birth rate among Latinas was almost twice the national average (National Campaign to Prevent Teen Pregnancy 1999). Hispanic women are moreover disproportionately represented among AIDS cases in the US. Although Hispanic women aged 15 and older represent just 7% of the US female population, they account for 20% of cumulative female AIDS cases (CDC 1999). In an effort to understand these health statistics, researchers have explored both demographic (e.g. poverty, discrimination, barriers to heath care) and cultural factors.

Although some scholars critique depictions of traditional Latin cultures for being stereotypical and invalid (e.g., Amaro 1988; De La Cancela 1989; Singer et al. 1990), there is also agreement about a number of shared cultural values (Marin 1988, 1989; Taylor 1996) that are likely to be important influences on family socialization practices. These include *familismo*, an emphasis on the family as the primary source of social support and identity, and *respeto*, the need to maintain respectful hierarchical relationships.

Another set of cultural beliefs relevant to the socialization of daughters in particular pertains to the importance of virginity until marriage. Within Latino families much of the socialization of daughters is influenced by historical beliefs in religion and family codes of honor. Historical religious influences led to a high value for female chastity; violation of this value resulted in dishonor for both the individual woman and her family (Espin 1984/1997). Because chastity of women within a family was one avenue through which honor was attained for the family as a whole, families vigorously safeguarded the virginity of unmarried women.

Other cultural beliefs relevant to sexual socialization include traditional gender role expectations and norms that promote female reticence and lack of knowledge about sexuality (for a review, see Raffaelli and Suarez-Al-Adam

1998). These long-standing beliefs about female sexuality often conflict with conditions encountered by Latino families in the US and are likely to be most salient as daughters enter adolescence. It has been suggested that the value of virginity may become a focal concern for some Latino parents who view US women as being promiscuous and link becoming 'Americanized' with being sexually promiscuous (Espin 1984/1997).

Prior research has identified specific cultural values and norms related to sexuality among Latino families, but the way that these beliefs influence the sexual socialization of children and adolescents remains largely unexplored (Barkley and Mosher 1995; Hurtado 1995). One study of 10–15 year old Puerto Rican and Mexican girls and their mothers (Villaruel 1998) revealed that to maintain daughters' virginity, families often established rules regarding dating and contact with males and tried to keep daughters close to home. Similar patterns have been reported by clinicians who work with Latina adolescents (Espin 1984/1997).

Other researchers have found that Latino parents are often reluctant to give their daughters information regarding sexuality (Darabi and Asencio 1987; Baumeister et al. 1995; Marin and Gomez 1997), communicating less about sexual topics than parents of other ethnic groups (CDC 1991). This lack of information and experience leads Latinas to be less knowledgeable about their own sexual anatomy and the basic physiological aspects of sexuality than non-Latino women (Barkley and Mosher 1995; Marin and Gomez 1997).

This body of research suggests that aspects of traditional culture influence sexual socialization in Latino families, but the small number of studies conducted to date limits conclusions that can be drawn. Moreover, prior research has not examined how specific parenting practices emerge from cultural beliefs, or how families negotiate a balance between old and new cultures. In an effort to add to the knowledge base about how Latino families socialize their daughters, the current analysis examined family experiences related to sexuality in a sample of adult Latinas who were interviewed about their experiences while growing up. We were particularly interested in examining how parental beliefs and values were enacted in everyday interactions around issues connected to sexuality and dating.

METHODS

PROCEDURES AND PARTICIPANTS

The study drew on an opportunity sample of Latina/Hispanic women who responded to mailings to Latino faculty and staff at a large Midwestern University or to informational flyers posted in public locations. Several participants also referred friends who subsequently participated. Recruitment materials targeted 20 to 45 year old Latino/Hispanic women who had grown up in Spanish-speaking families but had lived in the US for at least 8 years. After providing informed consent, women took part in individual in-depth interviews conducted in English by the first author. Participants received $20 for taking part in the study to cover their time, transportation, and childcare costs.

Twenty-two women had complete data and are included in the analyses (two additional women were excluded due to equipment problems that resulted in inaudible tapes). The average age of the sample was 31.2 years (median 27 years; range 20–45). Two-fifths (41%) of the respondents had never been married, 41% were currently married, and 18% were separated or divorced. Two (9%) of the women reported no religious affiliation; 68% were Catholic and 23% reported other religious affiliations.

All of the respondents had graduated from high school; 32% had attended college but not graduated; 18% had graduated from college; and 18% had postgraduate education. In contrast, parental levels of education were lower; over half of the respondents' fathers (57%) and mothers (55%) had not graduated from high school, with the majority of these parents leaving school by the ninth grade. A number of parents had graduated from high school (14% of fathers, 23% of mothers) and the remainder had attended or graduated from college (29% of fathers, 23% of mothers).

All respondents self-identified as Latino/Hispanic; 16 (73%) were of Mexican origin or descent and the remainder were from other Latin American or Caribbean countries. In terms of generation of immigration, the majority ($n = 19$) had been born in the US. Eleven (50%) of the women had at least one parent born outside the US (in ten cases, Mexico) and the remaining 11 had two US-born parents. Only three of the respondents had two US-born grandparents; the rest had one or both grandparents born outside the US.

Participants had high levels of current acculturation based on language. All interviews were conducted in English. In addition, current language use was assessed using a modified version of the Marin short acculturation scale (Marin et al. 1987). Respondents indicated which language they typically think in and use with their partner, friends, and at work on a three-point scale (1 = mostly or only Spanish, 2 = Both equally, 3 = mostly or only English). Responses were averaged to form an overall acculturation score; the average score was 2.59 (SD = 0.51). Two fifths ($n = 9$) of the women had an average of three (indicating English only), half ($n = 11$) were more or less bilingual (scores between 2.25 and 2.75), and two (9%) scored under 2.0 on the 3-point scale.

MEASURES

The interview guide consisted of open-ended and structured questions dealing with three main topic areas. The first area was sexual socialization within the family of origin, including gender role socialization (e.g., How did your parents teach you about how girls and boys 'should' behave? Do you remember any specific examples? Did your parents ever get angry or upset when you didn't behave in a certain way?), sexual communication (e.g., Did your parents ever talk to you about sex? What did they tell you about sex?), and reactions to the daughter's emerging sexuality (e.g., Tell me about when you started developing physically. What did your parents say/do?). The second area was early romantic and sexual experiences, including parental rules and messages about dating (e.g., When were you allowed to date or go out with boys?

What kinds of rules did your family have about dating? What did your parents tell you about boys? Did you ever get in trouble for breaking the rules?). The final area was sexuality-related beliefs, attitudes, and behavior, including pregnancy history, contraceptive use, and lifetime partners.

At the start of the interview, the investigator discussed how the project fit into her larger research program, and emphasized the exploratory nature of the work. Respondents were told that their role was not simply to provide answers but to help the investigator figure out what the questions were; that is, they were treated as co-participants in the research process and enlisted as collaborators in making meaning of their experiences. Thus, although the interview protocol was used as a guide and all women were asked the same core of questions, not all questions were asked in the same order and some interviews ranged into additional areas. Interviews averaged an hour to an hour and a half and were audio-taped.

DATA CODING AND ANALYSIS

Responses to open-ended questions were transcribed professionally, checked for accuracy by trained research assistants, and corrected. This procedure yielded over 400 pages of interview transcripts that were coded in two stages. First, transcripts were reviewed by two independent coders to locate specific segments that dealt with the focal domains addressed in the interview guide (i.e., parental concerns regarding dating, communication about sexual issues, family rules about dating, and actual dating and sexual experiences). Coders compared notes, identified discrepancies, and resolved them by discussion. These broad themes were then marked in a qualitative data analysis program (QSR NUD.IST) and the relevant portions of the interviews were extracted and reviewed by two coders to identify emergent themes within each of the focal domains. These themes were coded in the data analysis program, and patterns of responses across respondents tabulated. Responses to structured questions were entered into an SPSS data file and analyzed using quantitative analysis techniques.

RESULTS

The current analysis examines four domains related to adolescent sexual socialization: parental concerns regarding dating, family communication about sexual issues, family rules about dating, and actual dating experiences and early sexual behavior. The major sub-themes that emerged from the interview transcripts are listed in Table 1 (themes that were mentioned by fewer than five respondents are omitted from the table).

PARENTAL CONCERNS

All the respondents described parental concerns regarding interactions with boys and men during adolescence. A major cause for concern stemmed from parental mistrust of males, as several women described:

TABLE 1
Major themes identified in content analysis

PARENTAL CONCERNS
  Mistrust of Males/Daughter
  Concerns about Sexual Behavior/Pregnancy
  Image in Community
  Violation of Traditional Courtship Norms
  Safety

COMMUNICATION
  Lack of open communication
  Indirect communication of expectations

PARENTAL RULES ABOUT DATING
  Behavioral Restrictions
  Age Limitations
  Location Restriction
  Curfew
  Group Dating

DATING BEHAVIOR
  Avoidance of Dating
  Secret Dating
  Tension Surrounding Dating

> I think [mother] was real concerned about whether or not we would be taken advantage of . . . I always wondered was it that she didn't trust us or she didn't trust them and I think it was more she didn't trust them. (Lupe, 41)

> [Father] would just say it's not appropriate . . . for a girl to do that. Um, you need to be a certain age, um, boys can try certain things on you. I just want to keep you safe. (Antonia, 26)

Mistrust of males was linked to fear of premarital pregnancy, which was described as a parental concern by a number of participants:

> My friends attest he [father] would give us all lectures about how, you know, we can't let boys get in our way, because boys are bad and boys are, you know, just, they just want one thing and whatever I do don't get pregnant and that was just, I mean I would leave and "We don't want you coming home pregnant" . . . it was just whatever you do don't be pregnant or whatever you do don't get pregnant. (Silvia, 21)

> My mom spent a lot of time saying things to me like, "You'd better not get pregnant," even though I had no idea how you got pregnant at the time she was saying these things to me. If she had only known I was very naïve, she would have never even had to say those things, but she made it a point to always say those things to me and so of course I was afraid to do anything, so, cause I thought well, "God, what, what will she do to me if I do get pregnant?" because some-

times she'd threaten to send me away if I did certain things like get pregnant or, you know, just didn't do what she said, she would threaten to send me away, so I thought she would so I didn't do anything, just stayed home a lot. (Gloria, 41)

Several respondents also mentioned that their parents worried about how a daughter's behavior might affect the family's image in the community. Sandra (aged 40) explained that she was not allowed to date because "we came from a pretty good family, and so it would be a disgrace if anything . . . you know." Another respondent described her father's reaction when she brought a boyfriend to church:

When I talked to my father after the mass, he was kind of upset, he was like, he didn't want me to bring any of my boyfriends there. He said, "Unless, until you're married I don't want you bringing your boyfriends around," because he didn't want the community to get the idea that I was promiscuous or dating around. (Victoria, 24)

Similarly, Yolanda (27) said that her father

did not want to know who the guys [his daughters dated] were . . . if we're gonna get married, that's when he wants to know who our boyfriend or fiancé is. But other than that, he didn't want to know who our boyfriends are. Didn't want to see us with one guy and then another and another.

Thus, to many parents, daughters' dating behavior was seen as a potential source of embarrassment because it might expose the family to shame in the community.

Another reason for parental concern about dating was that US-style dating violated traditional patterns of courtship and marriage. Teresa (45) described the situation she experienced growing up in a predominately Mexican-American neighborhood:

If the guys wanted to court you they would be outside. You would be outside the house and you just talked, there was no such thing as you went to the car and you took off, you know, you wanted to talk to somebody you would be outside the house and then your parents would tell you, you have to come in and that was it, but it was no kissing or holding hands or nothing, actually it was just talking, getting to know each other actually until you decided whether you wanted to get married and then . . . the guy would have to tell whoever the parent was then, ask for your hand in marriage.

Similarly, when asked about her family's rules regarding dating, Yolanda (27), whose family moved from Mexico to the US when she was a young child, said:

This is what [my father] would tell us. Okay, you turn 15 and you have a coming out party. The two older sisters had that and then the rest of the girls didn't.

[We were] supposed to be able to date at the age of 15 and dating to him or to my mother was [the boy] comes here, you know, your window and then you just talk through the window . . . You know, no touching, no holding their hands and nothing like that.

The tension between traditional courtship styles and the reality of life in the US was expressed by one 26 year old woman's description of conversations with her Mexican-born father, who moved to the US before she was born:

I have asked him before, I've said, so, Dad, do you think that, that it is appropriate for us to go ahead and have boyfriends, to find out if this is the person that we want to marry, you know, how else are you going to find out if this is the person that you're going to marry, unless you meet this person, go out with this person, and so on the one hand it's like, you know, ah, intellectually he knows, okay, yeah, that makes sense, but it's almost as if though his social upbringing, you know, his, ah, it keeps him back from, you know, it's kind of like he's in between, you know, he's here in the United States, but yet he has all of this stuff that has told him that women are not allowed to go out with boyfriends. (Rosita, 26)

Silvia (21 years old) said her stepfather had begun pressuring her to be married because "according to him whenever I get married is when he can stop worrying. . . . It means I'll be in another household . . . and I'm no longer his worry, he doesn't, you know, I'll be taken care of."

COMMUNICATION ABOUT SEXUAL ISSUES

Respondents were asked about family communication about different sexual topics, including menstruation, physical development, facts about sex, morality, appropriate behavior, and boys/dating. The overall experience reported by study participants was for limited discussions about "biological" topics accompanied by extensive communication about the dangers of sexual activity. Only six (27%) of the respondents had discussed physical development with their parents, and eight (36%) had talked about the "facts of life" (i.e., intercourse and pregnancy). The most commonly discussed "biological" topic was menstruation, which fifteen (68%) of the women had discussed with a parent. In contrast, the majority of women had discussed appropriate behavior ($n = 20$; 91%), boys and dating ($n = 18$; 82%) and moral aspects of sexuality ($n = 13$; 59%).

Parental expectations about sexuality often took the form of warnings or prohibitions. For example, when asked if there were any rules she had to follow when she went out, Gabriela (27) responded, "don't let a guy, don't let a boy touch me." Inez (23) reported:

I do remember, I'm not sure exactly when it was, but I imagine probably when I was still in grade school my mother telling us that both her and my father were virgins when they got married and that's how it should be.

Other respondents described parental messages that were much more indirect:

> They would just give me some vague directions and then I think kind of expected me to fill it in. A lot of it was "You know what we expect from you" . . . it's basically understood . . . it's understood that you don't have sex before you're married. (Antonia, 26)

> I think it was comments, you know, that you would hear about, you know, I had an aunt who got pregnant and, and how that was so shameful. I mean it was just awful, you know, how could she do that. . . . [There was] always the recognition that there were good girls and bad girls and, you know, the talk about them and it wasn't just mother, it was the aunts, the tias, that would sit around and . . . you'd sit there and you . . . heard them talk . . . so the message was very clear, very indirect, but very clear that, that was not acceptable. (Lupe, 41)

The bulk of family communication focused on avoidance of sexual involvement, with few families providing information about sexuality or physical development.

FAMILY RULES ABOUT DATING

Parental concerns about their daughters' premature or inappropriate romantic and sexual involvement led to the implementation of a number of strategies to protect daughters. In some cases, parents attempted to shield their daughters from male attention by prohibiting the use of make-up or revealing clothes. One woman described how her Mexican-born father reacted to her and her sisters' adolescence:

> He didn't want us to wear make up or shave our legs, I can remember times when he would check my sisters' and my legs to see if we were shaving them . . . and he was just really, really cautious about us talking to guys and just growing up and becoming you know, puberty stage and just actually becoming women. Urn, he's a good father though. He's, he's been supportive as far as our education. Sure there were times when he ah, he threatened not to let us go to school anymore if, you know, we kept doing, you know, saying things that he didn't want us to do. (Yolanda, 27)

Some parents did not allow daughters to have social contact with males, as Silvia (21) succinctly described when asked what her parents' rules about social life were: "No boys." Similarly, when Victoria (24) was a teenager her father told her "he didn't want us to go out with, ah, to date, and he didn't want us to bring anyone, any boys to the house. That was a definite no." Another woman described her experience as follows:

> I was absolutely to do nothing. I came home from school with my school work and that was it. I didn't dare ask to go to games, movies, cause I just had to be

home. . . . I would try, I tried once or twice. And after that it was like "NO." . . .
I think they didn't trust me. So I thought what have I done that you don't trust
me. Obviously I couldn't have done anything, so it was like that. I stopped asking. If I had to stay at home, I had to stay at home. (Sandra, 40)

Parents used a variety of tactics to monitor their daughters' romantic activity. One strategy was to set an age before which daughters were not allowed
to date. When asked whether their parents had rules about the age at which
dating was allowed, eight women (38%) said they were not supposed to date
while living at home, nine (43%) were expected to wait until after age 15, and
four (19%) said no explicit age limits were set. In a number of cases, group or
chaperoned dates were permitted, but one-on-one dating was not.

Parents also restricted the locations where social interactions occurred.
For example, some respondents were allowed to interact with boys or men in
public or at social gatherings at which parents and relatives were present (e.g.,
weddings or community dances):

I was never allowed to have any boys in the house. . . . They didn't allow me to
go to other people's houses. It had to be public, you know, a dance or a picnic or
public thing. (Carmen, 45)

They knew that I was going out and that, you know, there were boys there and
so I guess in their minds it was, you know, they were at ease if it was I public,
because nothing could happen in public, but if you were at home God knows
what could happen. (Silvia, 21)

Parental rules about dating reflected the expectations that parents held for
their daughters. Overall, the "script" for adolescent sexuality was characterized by delayed and circumscribed romantic involvement on the part of their
daughters, with the ultimate goal being marriage. However, actual dating
and sexual behavior described by respondents often deviated from this ideal,
resulting in familial and personal stress.

DATING AND SEXUAL BEHAVIOR

Respondents reported a wide variation in their adolescent dating experiences.
Six (29%) began dating by age 14, ten (48%) by age 15 or 16, and five (24%) did
not date until age 17 or older. The average age at which respondents began
dating was 15.7 years, with early dating experiences often occurring without
parental knowledge or permission.

Parental expectations that daughters would not date resulted in some respondents waiting until they left home to have boyfriends. Olivia (25), who
was born in Mexico and moved to the US as a young child, described her
situation:

Because you're a girl you can't date until a certain age and there never really was
a real idea of what age you were supposed to be, because the whole time I was in

high school or even in college coming back home you couldn't date, because you were at home and that's not why you come home and so I always thought how are we supposed to get married if we can't even meet somebody?

In other cases, daughters engaged in covert dating to circumvent parental restrictions. About half of the respondents said they had dated without parental permission. For example, when asked about when she started dating, Lupe (41) replied, "the end of my sophomore year and it was sneak dating." Similarly, other women described their involvement in covert dating activities:

In 8th grade, I snuck out, well, I didn't sneak out, I went with a girlfriend to the movies but my Mom didn't know we were meeting up with two guys and I got in trouble for that. (Antonia, 26)

I can recall as a senior in high school, ah, sneaking out, cause by that time I had my car and, ah, a driver's license, so I'd wait until my parents went to bed and then I'd sneak out and sometimes I'd get in trouble for that. (Inez, 23)

At that point I had learned just, I tried to avoid my Dad and I tried to avoid my Mom and just tried to do as much as I could without letting them know about anything. (Silvia, 21)

Several other respondents said their mother helped them go out without their father's knowledge, as Olivia (25) described:

She would like lie for us to my Dad, so that we could do maybe like a high school social kind of thing also if we had dates or whatever if she knew the guy she would tell my dad that we were working and let us to go out for a little bit, or send one of us to chaperone.

In other families open dating was allowed but was surrounded with an atmosphere of tension and distrust. When Juanita (44) and her sisters came home after their curfew "[m]y Mom used to call us names . . . you know, bad names . . . she would just, using a Spanish word, she called us sluts and stuff like that." Other parents made their displeasure felt in less obvious ways:

Up to when I was a senior, I probably only had four dates and my Mom was not very nice to these poor boys when they came to my house, it was so embarrassing to me that I never did it until probably the middle of my senior year. (Gloria, 41)

Because of parental suspicion and displeasure, for many women dating was a source of tension and guilt. Of the 22 women interviewed, only a handful described their parents as supportive of their adolescent dating experiences.

Despite parental attempts to protect their daughters from premarital sexual involvement, 19 of the 22 respondents had engaged in premarital sexual intercourse. The mean age of sexual initiation was 18.2 years (SD = 3.7, range 12–28). Eleven of these 19 respondents did not use birth control the first time they had sex. A number of the women attributed their non-use of birth control to their ignorance about sex. Juanita (44), who became involved at 16 with a man in his 20s (and became pregnant the next year by another man), describes her early sexual encounters:

> I told him we weren't going to have sex if we didn't use something and he said, "Oh, I'll take care of it" and he didn't. . . . I was so naïve or dumb or something that I thought, you know, he's doing something . . . he's taking care of it.

Similarly, Isadora became pregnant at 17 by her first sexual partner, a 21 year old man who told her, "Oh, come on, nothing is going to happen the first time." Of the 19 women who had sexual experience, six (32%) became pregnant soon after they began having sex.

Although the direct links between early family environment and eventual dating and sexual experiences could not be examined systematically due to sample size limitations, a number of the respondents talked about having difficulties dealing with relationships as a result of their upbringing. Many of the women reported feeling guilty after their first sexual experience, because having sex was a "betrayal" of their family's values and expectations. Yolanda (27), who had sex with a 16 year old boy when she was 12 years old, said that she "had broken every rule that my Mom and Dad were trying to raise me with" and felt so guilty that she did not date until years later, when she was in college. Lupe (41) said that "I really think that I lived most of my adolescent life in fear that either God would get me or my parents in terms of behavior, specifically sexual." Rosita (26), who was not allowed to have boyfriends while living at home and was not sexually active at the time of the interview, reflected on the experiences of her older sisters, who both became pregnant soon after initiating sexual relations as young adults:

> I do really think that had an effect on us when we were growing up because my sisters, the first time that they went out . . . pretty much I want to say on a serious relationship [became pregnant] so to me that's telling me, OK, part of that is it could be because they were not allowed to have boyfriends when they were younger therefore now when you finally get to this point where you can have a boyfriend this is very serious.

DISCUSSION

The goal of the current study was to examine how sexual socialization practices in Latino families emerge from cultural values and to begin exploring how early experiences influence the later sexual behavior of Latinas. To integrate the findings, we draw on the framework of scripting theory, which holds that sexual behavior results from the interplay between cultural scenarios, interpersonal scripts, and intrapsychic scripts (Simon and Gagnon 1986, 1987).

Cultural scenarios provide the basic framework for sexual interactions, delineating the roles and possible actions of individuals in a sexual encounter. The cultural scenarios espoused by many of the respondents' parents depicted adolescent women as sexually vulnerable and in need of protection. All of the women in the study said their parents expressed concerns regarding interactions with boys and men. Reasons for parental concern included mistrust of males, fear of premarital pregnancy, concern about how a daughter's behavior might be viewed by members of the community, and the fact that US-style dating conflicted with "traditional" patterns of courtship and marriage. Parental expectations regarding their daughters' involvement in romantic activity can be seen in the fact that nearly two-fifths (38%) of the respondents said they were not supposed to date while living at home and over two-fifths (43%) said they were expected to wait until after they turned 15. Interestingly, 15 is the age at which the traditional coming-of-age ceremony for Latina girls, the *quinceañera*, is held (Davalos 1996; Cantu 1999). Also consistent with traditional Latin culture, female romantic involvement outside of marriage was described as dishonorable to the family, and many parents expressed a desire to maintain traditional courtship patterns even when they were aware that those behaviors were not typical of the larger society. Similar cultural norms have been reported in other research with Latino families (Espin 1984/1997; Villaruel 1998). However, cultural norms reflect ideals that may or may not be reflected in actual behavior. The current study extends prior research by identifying specific ways that parental concerns were manifested during their daughters' adolescence, which has implications for the development of interpersonal and intrapsychic scenarios.

According to scripting theory, interpersonal scenarios develop from an individual's actual experience in romantic and sexual situations. The women in the current study described family experiences that limited the degree to which they could engage in romantic or sexual behaviors as adolescents. Parents used a variety of tactics to curtail their daughters' sociosexual involvement, including restricting the age at which daughters were allowed to date, monitoring their clothes and use of make-up, and permitting heterosexual interactions only in specific locations or circumstances. Parental expectations that daughters would not date during early adolescence resulted in over half the respondents engaging in "sneak dating." Moreover, many respondents described the gap between parental expectations and actual dating practices as a source of conflict and tension. Also of relevance to the formation of interpersonal scenarios was the low level of family communication regarding sexuality. Less than one quarter of respondents had discussed the 'sexual facts and physiology' with their parents, echoing what has been reported in prior research (Pavich 1986; Soto 1983; Darabi and Asencio 1987; de Anda et al. 1990; Baumeister et al. 1995; Marin and Gomez 1997). Parental messages were most often centered on the importance of not having sex, with little information being provided on how to avoid sexual involvement or prevent negative sexual outcomes. Based on these analyses, we speculate that family practices related to sexuality have important implications for the intrapsychic scripts formed by women. Women who conformed to parental restrictions on sexual experimentation reported later relationship difficulties due to their inexperience, whereas women who rebelled against parental restrictions described feelings of guilt. Similar tensions regarding sexual choices among Latinas have been described by Espin (1984/1997), who works primarily with clinical populations.

The current analysis provides some hints about why US Latinas may be at increased risk of negative sexual outcomes (e.g., elevated rates of teenage pregnancy and HIV/AIDS infection) compared to women from other ethnic groups. As Espin (1984/1997) has noted, immigrant and ethnic minority groups may preserve aspects of their traditional culture related to sexuality long after they have adopted other aspects of the host culture. Although parental adherence to traditional values and restriction of daughters' sexual opportunities have potential benefits in terms of protecting daughters from negative outcomes, there are also potential risks to this strategy. In industrialized societies, individuals are expected to set limits on their sexual behavior without many of the external restraints that characterize 'traditional' societies (e.g., arranged marriages, gender segregation) (Brooks-Gunn and Paikoff 1997). As a result, the teenage years represent a crucial time "to practice managing sex and gender" (Thompson 1994, 219), as individuals are exposed to romantic and sexual situations in an age-graded fashion.

Our analysis suggests that many Latinas have limited romantic and sexual experience prior to leaving home. If traditional marriage arrangements were maintained, this limited experience would not be problematic. However, given the courtship patterns now prevalent in the US, Latinas are faced with the task of negotiating sexual encounters when they eventually do leave home, and they may be ill-equipped to do so. The women in the current study were highly educated (all had graduated from high school and most had some post-secondary education), yet over one half did not use birth control the first time they had sex and nearly one third had an unplanned pregnancy. The exploratory analysis described in this paper suggests that to understand the sexual behavior of US Latinas, researchers must examine more closely sexual socialization within the family of origin and take parents' culturally-influenced beliefs and practices into account.

LIMITATIONS AND FUTURE DIRECTIONS

This study has a number of limitations that suggest directions for future research. One limitation is the retrospective nature of the data. Retrospective accounts are subject to distortions or inaccuracies and may not reflect current socialization patterns in Latino families. Future research could address these concerns by examining more directly socialization processes within families in which there are teenagers and young people. A second limitation is the small sample size, which precluded examination of sub-group differences due to such factors as age or acculturation and limits the extent to which we can draw conclusions about Latino families in general. Future research should be conducted to explore different socialization patterns due to country of origin, time in the US, and parental attitudes regarding sexuality and gender. Finally, the exploratory nature of the study only permitted descriptive analyses, and did not allow an examination of predictive relations among the study variables. The intent of the study was to explore family experiences related to sexuality and identify themes and patterns; this descriptive information provides a basis for future more quantitative research.

ACKNOWLEDGMENTS

This research was supported by grants to the first author from the University of Nebraska Research Council and the National Institutes of Mental Health. The authors thank Jennifer Crispo, Stephanie Hewitt, Lynn Marcus, Nicole Miller, Tammy Pfeifer, Katie Pickett, Julie Siepker, Kathryn Wilke, and Byron Zamboanga for their contributions to the project.

REFERENCES

Amaro, H. 1988. Women in the Mexican-American community: Religion, culture, and reproductive attitudes and experiences. *Journal of Community Psychology* 16:6–20.

Barkley, B. H. and E. S. Mosher. 1995. Sexuality and Hispanic culture: Counseling with children and their parents. *Journal of Sex Education and Therapy* 21:255–67.

Baumeister, L. M., E. Flores and B. V. Marin. 1995. Sex information given to Latina adolescents by parents. *Health Education Research* 10:233–39.

Brooks-Gunn, J. and R. Paikoff. 1997. Sexuality and developmental transitions during adolescence. In J. Schulenberg, J. L. Maggs and K. Hurrelmann (eds.). *Health Risks and Developmental Transitions during Adolescence* (Cambridge: Cambridge University Press), 190–219.

Burgental, D. B. and J. J. Goodnow. 1998. Socialization processes. In N. Eisenberg (ed.) *Social, Emotional, and Personality Development*, fifth edition, volume 3 (New York: Wiley), 389–462.

CDC 1991. Characteristics of parents who discuss AIDS with their children—United States, 1989. *MMWR* 40:789–91.

CDC 1999. *HIV/AIDS Surveillance Report*, 11(1) (Atlanta: Centers for Disease Control).

Cantu, N. E. 1999. La quinceañera: Toward an ethnographic analysis of a life-cycle ritual. *Southern Folklore* 56:73–101.

Casper, L. M. 1990. Does family interaction prevent adolescent pregnancy? *Family Planning Perspectives* 22:109–14.

Child Trends 2000. Trends in sexual activity and contraceptive use among teens. *Child Trends: Research Brief* [http://www.childtrends.org].

Darabi, K F. and M. Asencio. 1987. Sexual activity and childbearing among young Hispanics in the US. *SIECUS Report*, 15, 6–8.

Davalos, K. M. 1996. La quinceañera: Making gender and ethnic identities. *Fronteirs* 16:1011–27.

de Anda, D., R. M. Becerra and E. Fielder. 1990. In their own words: The life experiences of Mexican-American and white pregnant adolescents and adolescent mothers. *Child and Adolescent Social Work* 7:301–18.

De La Cancela, V. 1989. Minority AIDS prevention: Moving beyond cultural perspectives towards sociopolitical empowerment. *AIDS Education and Prevention* 1:141–53.

Espin, O. M. 1984/1997. Cultural and historical influences on sexuality in Hispanic/ Latin women: Implications for psychotherapy. In E. Espin (ed.) *Latina realities: Essays on Healing, Migration, and Sexuality* (Boulder: Westview), 83–96.

Fox, G. L. and J. K. Inazu. 1980. Patterns and outcomes of mother-daughter communication about sexuality. *Journal of Social Issues* 36:7–29.

Holtzman, D. and R. Rubinson. 1995. Parent and peer communication effects on AIDS-related behavior among US high school students. *Family Planning Perspectives* 27:235–68.

Hurtado, A. 1995. Variations, combinations, and evolutions: Latino families in the United States. In R. E. Zambrana (ed.) *Understanding Latino Families: Scholarship, Policy, and Practice* (Thousand Oaks, CA: Sage), 40–61.

Jaccard, J. and P. J. Dittus. 1993. Parent-adolescent communication about premarital pregnancy. *Families in Society* 74:329–43.

Jaccard, J., P. J. Dittus and V. V. Gordon. 1998. Maternal correlates of adolescent sexual and contraceptive behavior. *Family Planning Perspectives* 28:159–85.

Katchadourian, H. 1990. Sexuality. In S. S. Feldman and G. R. Elliott (eds.) *At the threshold: The Developing Adolescent* (Cambridge: Harvard University Press), 330–51.

Marin, B. 1988. *AIDS Prevention in Non-Puerto Rican Hispanics* (Rockville: NIDA).

Marin, B. V. 1989. Hispanic culture: Implications for AIDS prevention. In J. Boswell, R. Hexter and J. Reinisch (eds.) *Sexuality and Disease: Metaphors, Perceptions, and Behavior in the AIDS Era* (New York: Oxford University Press), pp. 1–26.

Marin, B. V. and C. A. Gomez. 1997. Latino culture and sex: Implications for HIV prevention. In J. Garcia and M. Zea (eds.) *Psychological Interventions and Research with Latino Populations* (Boston: Allyn and Bacon Inc), 73–93.

Marin, G., F. Sabogal, B. V. Martin, R. Otero-Sabogal and E. J. Perez-Stable. 1987. Development of a short acculturation scale for Hispanics. *Hispanic Journal of Behavioural Sciences* 9:183–205.

McDade, K 1993. How we parent: Race and ethnic differences. In J. C. K. et. al. (eds.) *American Families: Issues in race and ethnicity*, volume 30 (New York: Garland Publishing Inc.), 283–300.

Miller, B. C., J. K. McCoy, T. D. Olson and C. M. Wallace. 1986. Parental discipline and control attempts in relation to adolescent sexual attitudes and behavior. *Journal of Marriage and the Family* 48:503–12.

National Campaign to Prevent Teen Pregnancy. 1999. *Fact sheet: Teen pregnancy and childbearing among Latinos in the United States*. The National Campaign to Prevent Teen Pregnancy [http:// www.teenpregnancy.org].

Parke, R. D. and R. Buriel. 1998. Socialization in the family: Ethnic and ecological perspectives. In N. Eisenberg (ed.) *Social, Emotional, and Personality Development*, fifth edition, volume 3 (New York: Wiley), 463–552.

Pavich, E. G. 1986. A Chicana perspective on Mexican culture and sexuality. *Journal of Social Work and Human Sexuality* 4:47–65.

Raffaelli, M. and M. Suarez-Al-Adam. 1998. Reconsidering the HIV/AIDS prevention needs of Latino women in the United States. In N. L. Roth and L. K Fuller (eds.) *Women and AIDS: Negotiating Safer Practices, Care, and Representation* (New York: Haworth), 7–41.

Simon, W. and J. H. Gagnon. 1986. Sexual scripts: Permanence and change. *Archives of Sexual Behavior* 15:97–120.

———. 1987. A sexual scripts approach. In J. H. Geer and W. T. O'Donohue (eds.) *Theories of Human Sexuality* (New York: Plenum Press), 363–83.

Singer, M., C. Flores, L. Davison, G. Burke, Z. Castillo, K. Scanlon and M. Rivera. 1990. SIDA: The economic, social, and cultural context of AIDS among Latinos. *Medical Anthropology Quarterly* 4:72–114.

Soto, E. 1983. Sex-role traditionalism and assertiveness in Puerto Rican women living in the United States. *Journal of Community Psychology* 11:346–54.

Taylor, J. M. 1996. Cultural stories: Latina and Portuguese daughters and mothers. In B. J. R. Leadbeater and N. Way (eds.) *Urban Girls: Resisting Stereotypes, Creating Identities* (New York: New York University Press), 117–31.

Thompson, S. 1994. Changing lives, changing genres: Teenage girls' narratives about sex and romance, 1978–1986. In A. S. Rossi (ed.) *Sexuality Across the Life Course* (Chicago: University of Chicago Press), 209–32.

Udry, J. R. and B. C. Campbell. 1994. Getting started on sexual behavior. In A. S. Rossi (ed.) *Sexuality Across the Life Course* (Chicago: University of Chicago Press), 187–207.

Villaruel, A. M. 1998. Cultural influences on the sexual attitudes, beliefs, and norms of young Latina adolescents. *Journal of the Society of Pediatric Nurses* 3:69–79.

Language Barriers Surrounding Medication Use among Older Latinos

Jan E. Mutchler, Gonzalo Bacigalupe, Antonia Coppin, and Alison Gottlieb

INTRODUCTION

The growing diversity of the older population has prompted new concerns about health disparities and differential access to health care among racial and ethnic groups. One group of particular significance in this regard is Latinos. Recent projections indicate that the share of the 65 and over US population that is Hispanic will grow rapidly in coming years. By the year 2030, growth trajectories will result in Hispanics being second in size only to non-Hispanic Whites within the older population (US Bureau of the Census 2004). As a result, it is important that we develop an understanding of the process underlying health-related decisions and behaviors of older Latinos.

An important vehicle by which good health in later life may be maintained, and health problems may be corrected or managed, is the appropriate use of medications. Older people take a disproportionate share of all prescription medications (Fillenbaum et al. 1993), and polypharmacy (use of multiple drugs) occurs frequently (Haug and Ory 1987). Due to the linguistic and literacy characteristics of the older Latino population, analysts frequently suggest that poor English language skills among many older Latino health care recipients—coupled with poor or no Spanish language skills among most health care providers—result in inadequate health care for older Latinos (Clark, Sleath, and Rubin 2004; Lee, Batal, Maselli, and Kutner 2002; Ortiz and Fitten 2000). The implications for medication use of these potential linguistic barriers are virtually unknown.

The primary goal of this research project was to explore the factors shaping medication practices among older Latinos. In conducting this research,

Jan E. Mutchler, Gonzalo Bacigalupe, Antonia Coppin, and Alison Gottlieb: "Language Barriers Surrounding Medication-Use among Older Latinos," reprinted from *Journal of Cross-Cultural Gerontology*, vol. 22 (2007): 101–14.

we discovered that language and communication issues challenge older Latinos' efforts to obtain and use medications. Strategies reported by our informants for overcoming these challenges, uncovered during the data collection phase of the study, are discussed later in the article.

LITERATURE REVIEW

Although older Latinos experience somewhat lower rates of death than their non-Latino counterparts, most evidence points to a poorer health profile among the Latino elderly population than among other groups (e.g., Markides, Rudkin, Angel, and Espino 1997; Slump, Clark, Johnson, and Wolinsky 1997). Health deficits in the Latino population are traced in the literature to a combination of factors, including sociodemographic characteristics such as education level or insurance coverage, and contextual influences such as context and quality of care received (Smedley, Stith, and Nelson 2003). Special emphasis has been placed in the literature on the significance of language barriers in shaping access to care and health outcomes. A substantial share of the older Latino population faces difficulty in communicating verbally in English (Bacigalupe and Gorlier 2001; Mutchler and Brallier 1999), and many are not literate in English (Mutchler and Bruner-Canhoto 2000).

Linguistic barriers between patients and providers have been identified as representing an especially important challenge to the delivery of adequate care to many older Latinos. Language barriers in the clinical encounter may form an obstacle to effective patient-physician communication (David and Rhee 1998; Smedley et al. 2003; Weitzman, Chang, and Reynoso 2004) and are linked to poorer doctor-patient relationships (Ferguson and Candib 2002) as well as poorer patient satisfaction (Carrasquillo, Orva, Brennan, and Burstin 1999; David and Rhee 1998; Smedley et al. 2003). Difficulty communicating also serves as a barrier to managing illness and accessing health care (Flores 2000; Flores, Abreau, Olivar, and Kastner 1998; Ponce, Hays, and Cunningham 2005); for example, patients with limited English proficiency have been found to have fewer physician visits (Derose and Baker 2000; Fiseclla, Franks, Doescher, and Saver 2002), longer hospital stays (John-Baptiste et al. 2004), poorer understanding of chronic disease and self-care (Becker, Beyene, Newsom, and Rodgers 1998), and poorer adherence to treatment protocols (Smedley et al. 2003).

In contrast to the large number of studies focusing on language barriers in the medical encounter, few studies have examined medication practices associated with language use among older Latinos. Older Latinos use both prescription and over the counter (OTC) medications somewhat less frequently than the older population at large, despite their poorer health profile (Espino et al. 1998; Krauss, Machlin, and Kass 1999). Yet older Latinos may be at high risk for complications and reactions associated with use of medications, due in part to language barriers and literacy deficits (Espino et al. 1998). For example, individuals with limited English skills are more likely to report that the side effects of prescribed medications had not been explained to them (David and Rhee 1998). Thus language barriers between patient and provider result in poorer understanding of treatments, and poorer patient adherence to medication regimes.

An additional factor underlying the ways in which communication barriers shape health care and medication practices is the use of informal networks in health care settings and decision-making. Family networks are linked to health behavior in later life, particularly so among older members of minority groups (Bagley, Angel, Dilworth-Anderson, Liu, and Schinke 1995; Flack et al. 1995: Johnson et al. 1995). Family members are frequent participants in medical encounters (Prohaska 1998) and may be active in medical decision-making (Dill, Brown, Ciambrone, and Rakowski 1995). Among non-English speaking elders, bilingual family members and friends are recognized as intermediaries between health care providers and their patients. However, some concerns have been expressed about the extent to which informal interpreters such as family members provide accurate reporting (Flores et al. 2003; Smedley et al. 2003). Informal interpreters may provide incomplete or incorrect information, or may filter information in such a way as to restrict full participation of the patient in decision-making.

SUMMARY

Older Latinos have a poorer health profile than do non-Latino Whites, and experiences with medications may contribute to this health disparity. Although little information on medication practices of older Latinos is available, some evidence suggests that this group's practices and experiences diverge from those of the larger population. Experiences obtaining and using medications, similar to experiences in the medical encounter more generally, may be shaped in part by communication barriers commonly occurring between Latinos and health care professionals. The purpose of this study is to explore the ways in which language barriers shape experiences obtaining and using medications, and to learn about the strategies undertaken by older Latinos to overcome these barriers.

MATERIALS AND METHODS

To address the gaps in the literature surrounding medication use among older Latinos, we sought to explore the meanings older Latinos bring to medication use and to define preliminary questions for further research. Inasmuch as the information on factors associated with medication use among older Latinos is limited, with little theoretical guidance surrounding the role played by language in this process, we chose to conduct focus groups with a small number of target individuals ($N=36$).

The entire study, including consent forms and interview protocols, was approved by the IRB at our home institution before the recruitment stage. Our research team was interdisciplinary and included expertise in qualitative methodologies. At the outset, we formed an advisory group to provide feedback on each stage of the research process. The advisory group was composed of a social pharmacist holding advanced degrees in both sociology and pharmacy, with a research background in diversity in medication practices: a Latino researcher specializing in health issues within the older Latino population; and a methodologist specializing in the study of health and health outcomes. These individuals provided valuable advice regarding recruitment of subjects, data collection and analysis, including triangulation strategies.

To enhance the transferability of the results, a theoretical sampling frame oriented the configuration of the focus group participants' composition. In consultation with our research institutes, a number of study sites were identified. Within each location—community organizations serving elders and Latinos in eastern Massachusetts—study participants were recruited. To be eligible for participation in the study, individuals were required to be of Latino origin, 50 years of age or older, and a resident of eastern Massachusetts. Although recent immigrants to the area were not excluded (and, in fact, they were specifically recruited for one focus group), persons who were classified as visitors to the US were not included. Only community-residing individuals were selected as participants. Our targeted study locations were diverse in terms of characteristics of the Latino residents (including national origin, immigration patterns, and other demographic characteristics). This heterogeneity served the purpose of widening the discursive threads that were explored in the study and was also reflective of the composition of the interview groups. Four focus groups of 60–90 minutes were conducted between November 2001 and June 2002. The four groups included the following:

- Diabetics participating in a program for Latino patients (mixed gender)
- Attendees at a senior center (mixed gender)
- Recent (within 5 years) female immigrants at a community center
- Men at a community center

Focus group sessions were conducted in community facilities easily accessible to participants. Each participant received $30 in appreciation of his/her participation. The focus groups were conducted by one of the co-investigators, who is fluent in both Spanish and English. We found that although many of our participants reported that they spoke English well, all of them preferred to be interviewed in Spanish.

Prior to the first focus group, a focus group protocol, or list of topics to be covered in the focus group sessions, was developed by the investigators and refined in consultation with our advisory group. It was revised somewhat for each subsequent group based on what was learned in the previous interview (see Fig. 1 for complete focus group guide). The focus group discussions were preceded by a short self-administered questionnaire in order to collect basic demographic information about the participants. The questionnaire was translated to Spanish by two of the investigators whose first language is Spanish: participants were helped by interviewers to fill it out. Data collected through this questionnaire is included in Table 1.

Description of the Participants

As part of our study design, special efforts were made to include men among the participants, given known differences in health care behaviors between men and women and the difficulties associated with recruiting men for many studies. As well, efforts were made to ensure that at least half of the respondents were 65 and over, given the escalation of medication use that occurs in

Topics

- *Experiences with medicines*
- *Over the counter and prescription medicines—differences in strategies*
- *Use of informal networks in using medicines*
- *Language issues as they shape medicine usage*
- *Role of physicians and pharmacists in shaping medicine use*

1. **Tell me about the last time you used any medicine.**
   - What kind of medicine was it? [Is that a medicine that you need a prescription to get, or one that you can get on your own?] *Go for facts/ stories first and keep questions open ended until all participants had a chance to speak* (later on ask for clarifications, and lastly find explanations).
   - Tell me about any problems you had taking the medicine.
     - Did you understand what your medicine was for and how you were supposed to take it?
     - Were there written instructions on the package or bottle? Did you understand them?
     - Did anyone explain to you how you were supposed to take the medicine? Who? [Did any family or friends help you understand or decide what to do?]
     - What happened when you went to the store to get the medicine? [Did you talk to a pharmacist? Did you understand what the pharmacist said to you? Did you feel that the pharmacist understood you? Did any family or friends help you with this?]
     - How could your experience with getting and using that medicine have been improved?
     - If you had to obtain refills, did you do something different?
   - Why did you use it?
   - Tell me about anyone who helped you use or get that medicine. [Did any of your family members or friends help you? How about any doctors or pharmacists? Include: deciding about use, obtaining medicines.]

   If the conversation addresses primarily prescription medicines, revise the above and ask: Tell me about another time you used some medicine that you didn't need a prescription to get.

2. **In general, when you're deciding about what kind of medicine to use when treating a problem with your health that is new or unfamiliar to you,**
   - What kind of treatment are you most likely to try first? [Would you try over-the-counter medicines first, or medicines that you get from a doctor, or something else? Why is that?]
   - Which do you rely on more: family and friends, or doctors and pharmacists? Why is that?

   We ask the last questions as a way of evoking new stories or allowing people to reaffirm patterns that were developed earlier.

Figure 1. Focus group questions guide.

TABLE 1
Description of the Focus Group Participants (N=36)

Characteristic		
Gender	Men	28%
	Women	72%
Age	Range	51 to 82 years
	Median	65 years
Country of origin	Puerto Rico	47%
	Dominican Republic	22%
	Other (Argentina; Columbia; Cuba;	31%
	El Salvador; Guatemala; Honduras; Mexico)	
Years living in the		
US	Range	0.5–51 years
	Median	18 years
Level of education	Range	0–16+ years
	Median	6 years
Self-rated ability to		
speak English	None or almost none	44%
	A little	35%
	Acceptable to well	21%
Self-rated health		
status	En crisis; fatal; malo; poor; very bad	17%
	Fair, no muy bien; no may buena; poco normal	11%
	Bien, estable, good, normal, stable, regular	72%

later life. The sample description presented in Table 1 indicates that our efforts were reasonably successful. Consistent with the national origin representation in eastern Massachusetts, the largest share of the participants were from Puerto Rico with the next largest origin the Dominican Republic. Participants varied widely in terms of how long they had been living in the mainland United States, and most reported low levels of education. Nearly half reported poor English-speaking ability, but most regarded their health as quite good. As is the case for the majority of older individuals in the US, most reported taking one or more medications. Commonly listed conditions for which one or more medications were taken included diabetes; high blood pressure; high cholesterol; depression; and arthritis. Reelecting the health and welfare policy climate of Massachusetts, all but two participants reported that they were covered by some form of health insurance, and many indicated that their insurance included prescription medication coverage. Thus, economic barriers to obtaining medication were limited in their direct influence on behavior for all but a few of the participants.

All focus group sessions were audiotaped with permission from the participants. Taped interviews were transcribed and translated into English by a professional translation firm that specializes in translation and interpretation in medical and legal settings. The veracity of the transcripts was verified by two of the investigators whose first language is Spanish. The transcriptions were read carefully by all of the investigators and discussed in detail. Subsequently, the English transcriptions were analyzed with the aid of NVivo 2.0 qualitative software. Given that our research purpose was to explore themes relating to challenges associated with medication use among individuals with limited English language skills, key words and phrases relating to these issues dominated the coding effort. Coding was completed primarily by the senior author, with input, assistance, and secondary coding completed by the other authors. The team coded each phrase after utilizing open coding to define recurrent themes. Multiple themes surrounding obtaining and using medications were explored; for example, experiences talking with physicians about medications; experiences obtaining medications from pharmacies; and experiences dealing with concerns about side-effects and drug interactions. Some themes spanned these experiences; for example, themes relating to language barriers, feelings of being discriminated against, and the use of informal networks as a strategy for overcoming these multifaceted obstacles. It was not the purpose of our study to identify differences in experience between subgroups (e.g., between men and women). Given the exploratory nature of our data, we focused our coding efforts on themes that recur across groups.

We acknowledge that focus groups—perhaps especially within the context of an exploratory pilot study such as ours—cannot represent the full range of attitudes, beliefs, or experiences within a population. Our groups were selected with an eye toward capturing diversity in experiences, but they do not incorporate the full range of diversity within the older Latino population as a whole. We believe that our study reveals some important ideas and potential avenues of investigation that can be pursued through additional conceptual development and further research.

RESULTS

LANGUAGE IS A BARRIER IN DEALING WITH MEDICATIONS

Respondents told numerous stories about clinical settings in which language posed a problem for receiving care. In addition, stories like the following suggest that pharmacies, as well as clinical settings, may be a source of frustration for older Latinos:

> Every time I go to get the medicine, if I don't take someone along who speaks English, it's a problem. I have problems there. [Because no one speaks Spanish?] No, not at the pharmacy. Not at the pharmacy. . . . Since I don't understand, all they say to me is "No." I laugh and I leave because it's my fault, because why haven't I learned a little bit of English? And I leave, then I say to my son, "You go, because I don't understand that."

Another participant told a similar story,

> My husband used to have a lot of problems . . . when he got his prescription from the doctor and he went to pick up the medicine. Sometimes he would come

back with it [that is, the written prescription paper] in his pocket because he couldn't find anyone to help him.

These and similar stories suggest that challenges associated with limited English proficiency are not restricted to the clinical setting. Older individuals with limited English language skills encounter barriers to obtaining medications that reach far beyond the physician's office. A more holistic approach to remedying health disparities should take into account the behavior and interactions occurring among non-physician practitioners and pharmacy staff as well.

Language Issues Are Seen As Being Linked to Discrimination

Language barriers in medical settings were related to perceptions of discrimination on the part of the older Latinos in our study. The poor English skills shared by many of our respondents were seen as a source of ridicule and as an excuse for poor treatment by physicians and pharmacy staff. For example, in dealing with physicians:

> I felt very bad because . . . (the doctor) asked, "How long have you been here?" I said, so many years. "Well, why can't you speak English?" Because I came here to work, to raise my family, and time slipped by. I didn't know that was a sin. That's what I told him.

Similar experiences were reported in interactions at the pharmacy:

> In the pharmacy when they don't understand you, they give you dirty looks [she makes a blowing or sniffing sound]. And they go [loud sigh].

These stories suggest that for these older Latinos, limited English proficiency may serve as a barrier to forming respectful relationships with health care professionals.

Older Latinos Are Actively Involved in Their Health Choices

Despite these obstacles, the older Latinos with whom we spoke took active responsibility for their own health and health care. Most were reasonably knowledgeable about their health conditions; most expressed an interest in taking charge of their own care. These respondents reported that they paid close attention to their health conditions and reactions to medications, reporting any problems to their physicians:

> When they give me a new refill, for example, to know if they gave me the exact amount the doctor told me, I control that, whether they give me less pills or they give me more; I control all that. Because I have to report to the doctor. In fact, when I check my sugar I have to give the doctor a report of what the reading is every day. And I am very careful because I like myself very much.

In the discussions, the respondents' involvement in their own health care is frequently linked to their understanding of the medicines taken and their relationships with physicians:

> And when I see that a medicine is not producing the reaction I expected, I call the doctor and I say, "Look, I'm going to suspend this medicine; it's causing such and such a reaction." He immediately says, "Suspend it." Besides, a doctor isn't a magician, so I help them with things that are happening to me.

And, from another informant:

> I feel that if you are a patient and I have a good doctor, we should be friends, and talk about medicine. . . . In other words, it's my habit to talk to them and tell them. . . . I give them clues to my problem, too. I say, "Look, doctor," because I've dealt with doctors for a long time, and I've always been like that. Ever since I was young and started having my children, I have liked to talk to doctors about the problems and the medicines. And that has helped in the way they treat me.

These stories reinforce the value of good communication and trusting relationships for our older informants. The older individuals with whom we spoke are actively engaged in their health care and seek to make informed choices about medications. Comments made by those who have formed good relationships and successful strategies for communicating with providers suggest that good communication is a key to satisfactory health care experiences. For others, communication obstacles are problematic if they prevent full understanding and participation in decision-making.

OLDER LATINOS DEVELOP NUMEROUS STRATEGIES FOR MAXIMIZING THEIR UNDERSTANDING

A key goal of the study was to identify strategies by which language barriers surrounding the use of medications were overcome. According to our informants, using family and friends as interpreters and sources of help is a key strategy. Seeking out Spanish-speaking health care providers and pharmacies with Spanish-speaking staff was also frequently mentioned. Issues and challenges associated with using formal interpreters were also discussed.

In our discussions with older Latinos, family and friends were frequently identified as sources of assistance with medical concerns and as interpreters. With respect to helping with medical issues:

> I think I have always had my children take me. They take me because I can't do it alone.

Informal networks are also used to help deal with pharmacy staff, as another informant explains:

Yes, there are problems [at the pharmacy] because I don't speak English. Sometimes when—for example, last time, I had a cold and I had to take my uncle,
I said to him, "Let's go" so I can tell what the man is saying. It's the only way
because . . . the truth is, I don't understand him.

Moreover, family and friends are used on a day-to-day basis to translate the
directions on medications:

Over where I live there is a lady who knows a lot of English. I say to her. "Look,
you know English, please tell me what it says here." It has to be someone I know.
Or else I'll ask Maria, my daughter.

Respondents reported that they sought out Spanish-speaking physicians
to ease communication barriers. Many stories linked the Latino ethnicity
of their physician to the respondent's own feelings of confidence and com-
petence with respect to taking medicines. Respondents frequently reported
feeling knowledgeable about the medicines they were taking because their
doctors explained the issues thoroughly. For example:

I have a Hispanic doctor . . . who tells me for each medicine what each one is for.

And, from one particularly articulate informant:

Me, for example, I understand English well, I read it, I speak it and I prefer to
go to Hispanic doctors. Because I also believe there is a psychological affinity,
in addition to the rules code, I think there is a good feeling. . . . The security
one has when one has a simple knowledge, and that one is spoken to in Spanish
of the . . . of the people, because there are some who appear to have a doctor's
diploma above and they use the terms there of . . . [That can't be understood?]
Scientific terms and I say "well, look, speak to me in Spanish" so I can assimilate
it . . . and one can progress more, get better.

However, some respondents indicated that it was not necessary for the physician to be Latino him or herself for good understanding to be perceived.
Rather, speaking even a little Spanish led to feelings of understanding:

My doctor also explains what the medicine is for. [And does he explain it in
Spanish or in English?] In Spanish. My doctor isn't Hispanic but he speaks
Spanish.

And, from another participant,

[Tell me, does your doctor speak Spanish?] A little bit. [Do you speak English to
him?] No, Spanish. [Spanish—so how do you understand each other?] Because
he speaks some. That's the thing.

In the absence of a Spanish-speaking physician, use of formal interpreters is a familiar strategy reported by many respondents. For example:

> I walk to the hospital and they . . . I don't know much English and they get me an interpreter and I do all right.

However, the system for using formal interpreter services frequently provides less than optimal satisfaction. For example, another participant reports difficulties associated with using interpreters:

> When I have an appointment—not with my regular doctor because he speaks Spanish, but for my eyes or for some tests they are going to do or something—I have to wait two or three hours to get an interpreter. . . . And sometimes I have even missed doing what they were going to do that day because there is no interpreter.

Obtaining and effectively using pharmaceuticals requires more than just communication with a physician, however. As noted earlier, obtaining medicines at pharmacies is cited as a familiar challenge for those who do not speak English well. Our older Latino respondents typically had worked out strategies for obtaining medications that involved the use of informal networks and nonverbal communication. For example:

> Well, when my medicines run out, the 28th of this month, I have to order them the day before. So, since I live with my daughter, I say to my daughter, "Look, order the medicines for me from the pharmacy." And she orders them over the phone. So the next day, what I have to do is take the card of the Plan, and they look up the medicine for me right away and they give it to me. . . . I have to take the vial with me because since I don't speak English, by telephone I don't understand.

Other respondents sought out pharmacies with Spanish-speaking staff as a way to facilitate obtaining medications. For example, the woman reporting that her husband sometimes came home with the prescription papers still in his pocket, having been unable to find anyone to help him at the pharmacy, indicated that this problem was resolved with cooperation of his physician and with the hiring of Spanish-speaking staff:

> He says, "Well," he said to the doctor, "I have a problem with this. Why don't you call the pharmacy so that they will give it to me, or see what you can do about it?" So when he goes, what the doctor does is he calls the pharmacy to have them give the prescription to him. But they have a Hispanic girl there now.

and

> We're fortunate to go, in this pharmacy here in C. they speak Spanish. There's no problem. [Aha. Is there always someone there who speaks Spanish?] There's always someone. It's rare that someone isn't there.

Similarly,

> I get my medicine at [name of pharmacy] and they give me directions and everything in Spanish. [Aha, written?] Yes. written.

Thus, for this group of limited-English proficiency older Latinos, a variety of strategies are pieced together to solve the problem of communication barriers. When possible, Spanish-speaking physicians and pharmacy staff are preferred. However, informal strategies making use of bilingual family members and friends are common, as well as use of formal interpreter services.

Trust is a Key Component of Patient Decision-Making, and Trust is Related to Language

Throughout the interviews, it was evident that medication use is intrinsically linked to the relationship between patients and their providers, and especially to the level of trust developed between the two. For example, in describing two different interactions, this informant equates shared language with real communication:

> And thank God, that doctor is a doctor that people appreciate very much because she cares about her patients, she devotes time to you, she talks to you, she asks if there are any questions, she looks up your record, and things that you don't even remember, she says, "Look, what about this, how is this doing, how is that doing?". . . . I used to have another doctor before: that's why I switched. She didn't speak my language. She was a—you had an appointment and it was really quick. You left there like—the interpreter arrived and she said this and that and the other, and you left there without knowing. You had no means of communicating with her.

This respondent links the issues of respect and trust to language:

> I am very grateful to the doctors. They treat me with a lot of respect, a lot of caring, a lot of attention, because of the many problems I have, to avoid any complications. Despite the fact that I am Latina. But I get along with a doctor in English, too, thank God.

And, perhaps mostly directly, this informant highlights the important link between communication and trust in defining a successful relationship:

> I trust them, so they trust me too. . . . I help the doctors to control my problems too. I talk a lot with them.

The importance of a trusting and respectful relationship for these informants may form the basis for some dissatisfying experiences surrounding the use of formal interpreter services. According to our respondents, the veracity of the interpretation is sometimes doubted. Some of the older Latino

respondents report that they simply do not trust that the interpreter is providing an accurate account of what is being said.

> For the matter of my vision, I go with my daughter. Or with my son. . . . In these
> cases, it's better to take a family member because that way, you remove doubts
> of whether they are saying the truth or not.

Similarly, from another informant,

> Sometimes, you speak to a doctor through the interpreter and they don't tell
> the doctor what you said. They say something different. Because it has hap-
> pened to me many times. [And how do you know they're saying something
> different? Because you know some English?] I know English. And sometimes
> you say one thing and they say another thing. It has happened to me often, and
> I've heard from others, too.

For these informants, understanding and trusting is a critically important
part of a good relationship with a medical provider. Although interpreters
can help overcome some of the barriers to communication, they may not benefit from the formation of a trusting relationship, especially if the veracity of
the interpretation itself is in doubt.

DISCUSSION

Our study suggests that language barriers may have implications for medication choices and medication adherence on the part of older Latinos. Inasmuch as a great deal of medication use in later life surrounds the treatment
of chronic and potentially life-threatening conditions, this relationship may
be one source of health disparities between Latinos and non-Latinos and de-
serves additional scrutiny. In our discussions with older Latinos about their
medication use and health-seeking activities, language barriers were promi-
nently mentioned. These barriers were problematic because they hindered
our informants' understanding of their health conditions and of the medications prescribed. They were also problematic because they formed an obstacle
to developing a trusting and respectful relationship with health providers.
Seeking out Spanish-speaking physicians and pharmacies and using family
members and friends as informal interpreters were commonly used strategies designed to create better and more trustworthy understanding.

The participants in our group interviews provided insight into a process
relating to health seeking and taking medicines that is reflective and based
on active decision-making. Similar to the process described by Stoller, Forster,
and Portugal (1993), our older Latino informants are actively involved in their
care when making decisions about medicines. These decisions appear to be
linked to their understanding of the health conditions with which they are
dealing, and also with the relationships perceived by our informants with
their health providers. Similarly to that described by Stoller (1998), individual

response to symptoms or health experiences may be shaped by the "social interactions" surrounding illness and wellness.

How does language fit into this process? Our findings suggest that language is relevant neither exclusively as a proxy for cultural health beliefs, nor simply as a barrier to technical understanding of medical issues. Certainly, language does play a structural role in shaping medication practices: the reflective, personal assessment process surrounding medication use is necessarily based in part on the patient's understanding of her health condition and the treatment prescribed by the health provider. However, the role played by language appears to be more multidimensional. Indeed, language (and here, proficiency in English) could be construed as a relational dimension in which trust and respect play larger roles than does the literal understanding of the language. This is reflected in the extent to which language barriers are related to perceived discrimination or, conversely, perceived respect among the patient and health care providers, pharmacy staff, and others involved in health-seeking. It is also reflected in the extent to which information about health and medicines, and the sources of that information, are trusted. The quality of the relationship between our older Latino informants and their health advisors appears to shape the perceived trustworthiness of the information obtained from those advisors. This relationship quality may be strongly shaped by language and the perceived ability to communicate (see Weitzman et al. 2004, for similar conclusions).

Thus both *understanding* and *believing*, or trusting, are critical aspects of encounters between older Latino patients and providers. Direct communication with providers who speak the same language is preferred by our Latino informants, both because understanding is enhanced and because true communication and confidence in the information received is more likely. When direct communication is not possible because of language barriers, an intermediary is often used. Formal interpreters are familiar to our Latino informants, but are sometimes less preferred, primarily because they are considered to be less trustworthy sources, especially when they are not known to the informant. The use of family members or friends as interpreters is described more positively. The benefit to our informants of using informal interpreters is expressed both in terms of convenience (informal interpreters are often readily available) and in terms of trustworthiness (informal interpreters can be trusted to convey information more accurately, in the opinion of our informants).

We are reluctant to offer any strong conclusions based on this small, qualitative study of older Latinos in eastern Massachusetts. The health policy and health care climate within which our subjects are seeking services and medications may shape their experiences in ways that are not shared by Latinos in some other geographic areas. We do regard our findings as intriguing and warranting further examination. For example, if language barriers between patients and health providers inhibit compliance because patients do not trust the information received in medical encounters, strategies designed for clinical settings that focus purely on literal interpretation may not have the desired benefit. Alternative strategies that emphasize both understanding and trust may be required.

ACKNOWLEDGMENTS

We gratefully acknowledge the research grant support of National Institute on Aging Grant no. RO3 AG19857-01. This research was also supported in part by the Intramural Research program of the NIH, National Institute on Aging. We appreciate the insights and comments from Jeffrey Burr, Vanessa Calderon-Rosado, Brian Clarridge, Michael Montague, and two anonymous reviewers.

REFERENCES

Bacigalupe, G., and J. C. Gorlier. 2000. Latino Medicaid consumers' experiences: Obtaining health care and caring for their families health. Paper presented at the annual meetings of the American Public Health Association, November, Boston, MA.

Bagley, S., R. Angel, P. Dilworth-Anderson, W. Liu, and S. Schinke. 1995. Panel V: Adaptive health behaviors among ethnic minorities. *Health Psychology* 14:632–640.

Becker, G., Y. Beyene, E. Newsom, and D. Rodgers. 1998. Knowledge and care of chronic illness in three ethnic minority groups. *Family Medicine* 30:173–178.

Carrisquillo, O., E. J. Orva, T. A. Brennan, and H. R. Burstin. 1999. Impact of language barriers on patient satisfaction in an emergency department. *Journal of General Internal Medicine* 14:82–87.

Clark, T., B. Sleath, and R. H. Rubin. 2004. Influence of ethnicity and language concordance on physician-patient agreement about recommended changes in patient health behavior. *Patient Education and Counseling* 53:87–93.

David, R. A., and M. Rhee. 1998. The impact of language as a barrier to effective health care in an underserved urban Hispanic community. *Mount Sinai Journal of Medicine* 67:393–97.

Derose, K. P., and D. W. Baker. 2000. Limited English proficiency and Latinos' use of physician services. *Medical Care Research and Review* 57:76–91.

Dill, A., P. Brown, D. Ciambrone, and W. Rakowski. 1995. The meaning and practice of self-care by older adults: A qualitative assessment. *Research on Aging* 17:8–41.

Espino, D. V., M. J. Lichternstein, H. P. Hazuda, D. Fabrizio, R. C. Wood, J. Goodwin, et al. 1998. Correlates of prescription and over-the-counter medication usage among older Mexican Americans: The Hispanic EPESE study. *Journal of the American Geriatrics Society* 46:1228–34.

Ferguson, W. J., and L. M. Candib. 2002. Culture, language, and the doctor-patient relationship. *Family Medicine* 34:353–61.

Fillenbaum, G. G., K. T. Hanlon, E. H. Corder, T. Ziquhu-Page, W. E. Wall, Jr., and D. Brock. 1993. Prescription and nonprescription drug use among Black and White community-residing elderly. *American Journal of Public Health* 83:1577–82.

Fiscella, K., P. Franks, M. P. Doescher, and B. G. Saver. 2002. Disparities in health care by race, ethnicity, and language among the insured: Findings from a national sample. *Medical Care* 40:52–59.

Flack, J., H. Amaro, W. Jenkins, S. Kunitz, J. Levy, M. Mixon, et al. 1995. Panel 1: Epidemiology of minority health. *Health Psychology* 14:592–600.

Flores, G. 2000. Culture and the patient physician relationship: Achieving cultural competency in health care. *Journal of Pediatrics* 136:14–23.

Flores, G., M. Abreau, M. Olivier and B. Kastner. 1998. Access barriers to health care for Lain children. *Archives of Pediatrics and Adolescent Medicine* 152:1119–25.

Flores, G., M. B. Laws, S. J. Mayo, B. Zuckerman, M. Abreau, L. Medina, and E. J. Hardt. 2003. Errors in medical interpretation and their potential clinical consequences in pediatric encounters. *Pediatrics* 111:6–14.

Haug, M. R., and M. G. Ory. 1987. Issues in elderly patient-provider interactions. *Research on Aging* 9:3–44.

John-Baptiste, A., G. Naglie, G. Tomlinson, S. M. H. Alibhai, E. Eetchells, A. Cheung, et al. 2004. The effect of English language proficiency on length of stay and in-hospital mortality. *Journal of General Internal Medicine* 19:221–28.

Johnson, K., N. Anderson, E. Bastida, B. Kramer, D. Williams, and J. Wong. 1995. Panel II: Macrosocial and environmental influences on minority health. *Health Psychology* 14:601–12.

Krauss, N. A., S. Machlin, and B. L. Kass. 1999. Use of health care services, 1996. Agency for Health Care Policy and Research. Research Finding no. 7. pub no. 99–0018. INTERNET: www.meps.ahcpr.gov/publicat.htm.

Lee, L. J., H. A. Batal, J. H. Maselli, and J. S. Kutner. 2002. Effect of Spanish interpretation method on patient satisfaction in an urban walk-in clinic. *Journal of General internal Medicine* 17:641–45.

Markides, K. S., L. Rudkin, R. J. Angel, and D. V. Espino. 1997. Health status of Hispanic elderly. In L. Martin and B. Soldo (eds.), *Racial and ethnic differences in the health of older americans* (pp. 285–300). Washington DC: National Academy.

Mutchler, J. E., and S. Brallier. 1999. English language proficiency among older Hispanics in the United States. *The Gerontologist* 39:310–19.

Mutchler, J. F., and L. Bruner-Canhoto. 2000. Health status and English proficiency among older Latinos. Paper presented at the annual meetings of the American Public Health Association. Boston, November.

Ortiz, F., and L. J. Fitten. 2000. Barriers to healthcare access for cognitively impaired older Hispanics. *Alzheimer Disease and Associated Disorders* 14:141–50.

Ponce, N. A., R. D. Hayes, and W. E. Cunningham. 2005. Linguistic disparities in health care access and health status among older adults. *Journal of General Internal Medicine* 21:786–91.

Prohaska, T. 1998. The research basis for the design and implementation of self-care programs. In M. G. Ory and G. H. DeFriese (eds.). *Self-care in later life: Research, program, and policy issues* (pp. 62–84). Berlin Heidelberg New York: Springer

Smedley, B. D., A. Y. Stith, and A. R. Nelson. (eds.) 2003. Unequal treatment: Confronting racial and ethnic disparities in health care. Washington DC: National Academy.

Stoller, E. P. 1998. Dynamics and processes of self-care in old age. In M. G. Ory and G. H. DeFriese (eds.). *Self-care in later life: Research, program, and policy issues* (pp. 24–61). Berlin Heidelberg New York: Springer.

Stoller, E. P., L. E. Forster and S. Portugal. 1993. Self-care responses to symptoms by older people. *Medical Care* 31:24–40.

Stump, T. E., D. O. Clark, R. J. Johnson, and F. D. Wolinsky. 1997. The structure of health status among Hispanic, African American, and White older adults. *The Journals of Gerontology* 52B (Special Issues), 49–60.

US Bureau of the Census. 2004. Projection of the total resident population by age, race, and Hispanic origin: 2000 to 2050. Population Projections Branch, Population Division. Washington. D.C.: US Census Bureau. Available online: www.census.gov/ipc/www/ usinterimproj.

Weitzman, P. F., G. Chang, and H. Reynoso. 2004. Middle-aged and older Latino American women in the patient doctor interaction. *Journal of Cross-Cultural Gerontology* 19:221–39.

Selected Bibliography

Aguilar-Gaxiola, Sergio A., with Thomas P. Gullotta, eds. *Depression in Latinos: Assessment, Treatment, and Prevention.* New York: Springer, 2008.

Aguirre-Molina, Marilyn, with Carlos W. Molina, eds. *Latina Health in the United States: A Public Health Reader.* San Francisco: Jossey-Bass, 2003.

Aguirre-Molina, Marilyn, with Carlos W. Molina, and Ruth Enid Zambrana, eds. *Health Issues in the Latino Community.* San Francisco: Jossey-Bass, 2001.

Becerra, Rosina M., with Marvin Karno, Javier I. Escobar, eds. *Mental Health and Hispanic Americans: Clinical Perspectives.* New York: Grune and Stratton, 1982.

García, Jorge G., with María Cecilia Zea, eds. *Psychological Interventions and Research with Latino Populations.* Boston: Allyn and Bacon, 1997.

Koss-Chioino, Joan D., with Luis A. Vargas. *Working with Latino Youth: Culture, Development, and Context.* San Francisco: Jossey-Bass, 1999.

LaVeist, Thomas A., ed. *Race, Ethnicity, and Health: A Public Health Reader.* San Francisco: Jossey-Bass, 2002.

Mishra, Shiraz I., with Ross F. Connner and J. Raul Magaña, eds. *AIDS Crossing Borders: The Spread of HIV Among Migrant Latinos.* Boulder, Colo.: Westview Press, 1996.

Molina, Carlos W., with Marilyn Aguirre-Molina, eds. *Latino Health in the United States: A Growing Challenge.* Washington, D.C.: American Public Health Association, 1994.

Organista, Kurt C. *Solving Latino Psychosocial and Health Problems: Theory, Practice, and Populations.* Hoboken, N.J.: John Wiley and Sons, 2007.

Santiago-Irizarry, Vilma. *Medicalizing Ethnicity: The Construction of Latino Identity in a Psychiatric Setting.* Ithaca, N.Y.: Cornell University Press, 2001.

Smith, Robert L., with R. Esteban Montilla, eds. *Counseling and Family Therapy with Latino Populations.* New York: Routledge, 2006.

Torres, Sara, ed. *Hispanic Voices: Hispanic Health Educators Speak Out.* New York: National League for Nursing Press, 1996.

Index

About the Editor
and Contributors

EDITOR

Ilan Stavans is Lewis-Sebring Professor in Latin American and Latino Culture and Five College–Fortieth Anniversary Professor at Amherst College. A native from Mexico, he received his doctorate in Latin American Literature from Columbia University. Stavans' books include *The Hispanic Condition* (HarperCollins, 1995), *On Borrowed Words* (Viking, 2001), *Spanglish* (HarperCollins, 2003), *Dictionary Days* (Graywolf, 2005), *The Disappearance* (TriQuarterly, 2006), *Love and Language* (Yale, 2007), *Resurrecting Hebrew* (Nextbook, 2008), and *Mr. Spic Goes to Washington* (Soft Skull, 2008). He has edited *The Oxford Book of Jewish Stories* (Oxford, 1998), *The Poetry of Pablo Neruda* (Farrar, Straus and Giroux, 2004), *Isaac Bashevis Singer: Collected Stories* (3 vols., Library of America, 2004), *The Schocken Book of Sephardic Literature* (Schocken, 2005), *Cesar Chavez: An Organizer's Tale* (Penguin, 2008), and *Becoming Americans: Four Centuries of Immigrant Writing* (Library of America, 2009). His play *The Disappearance*, performed by the theater troupe Double Edge, premiered at the Skirball Cultural Center in Los Angeles and has been shown around the country. His story *"Morirse está en hebreo"* was made into the award-winning movie *My Mexican Shivah* (2007), produced by John Sayles. Stavans has received numerous awards, among them a Guggenheim Fellowship, the National Jewish Book Award, an Emmy nomination, the Latino Book Award, Chile's Presidential Medal, and the Rubén Darío Distinction. His work has been translated into a dozen languages.

CONTRIBUTORS

Margarita Alegría, Center for Multicultural Mental Health Research, Cambridge Health Alliance, and Harvard University Medical School.

Gonzalo Bacigalupe, Graduate College of Education, University of Massachusetts, Boston.

Sharon Bzostek, Princeton University.

Glorisa Canino, University of Puerto Rico.

Zhun Cao, Center for Multicultural Mental Health Research, Cambridge Health Alliance, and Harvard University Medical School.

Antonia Coppin, Laboratory of Epistemology, Demography, and Biometry, National Institute of Aging, Bethesda, Maryland.

T. Elizabeth Durden, Bucknell University.

Noreen Goldman, Princeton University.

Bridget K. Gorman, Pennsylvania State University.

Alison Gottlieb, Gerontology Institute, University of Massachusetts, Boston.

Peter J. Guarnaccia, Institute for Health, Health Care Policy, and Aging Research, Rutgers University.

Nancy S. Landale, Pennsylvania State University.

Daniel Llánes, Pennsylvania State University.

Nora Mulvaney-Day, Center for Multicultural Mental Health Research, Camlridge Health Alliance, and Harvard University Medical School.

Jan E. Mutchler, Gerontology Institute, University of Massachusetts, Boston.

Lenna L. Ontai, University of Nebraska, Lincoln.

R. S. Oropesa, Pennsylvania State University.

Anne Pebley, University of California, Los Angeles.

Antonio Polo, DePaul University.

Marcela Raffaelli, University of Nebraska, Lincoln.

Patrick E. Shrout, New York University.

William Sribney, Third Way Statistics.

María Torres, Center for Multicultural Mental Health Research, Cambridge Health Alliance.

Doryliz Vila, University of Puerto Rico.

Anahí Viladrich, Urban Public Health Program, School of Health Sciences, Hunter College of the City University of New York.

Meghan Woo, Harvard University School of Public Health.